TEACHING THE HOLOCAUST

Related titles:

Dan Cohn-Sherbok: *Understanding the Holocaust*
Larry Kramer: *Reports from the Holocaust*
Robert Phillips: *History Teaching, Nationhood and the State: A Study in Educational Politics*
Gonzalo Retamal and Ruth Aedo-Richmond (eds): *Education as a Humanitarian Response*
Gabriele Rosenthal (ed.): *Holocaust in Three Generations: Families, Victims and Perpetrators of the Nazi Regime*
John Slater: *Teaching History in the New Europe*
John Wilson: *Key Issues in Education and Teaching*

Teaching the Holocaust
EDUCATIONAL DIMENSIONS, PRINCIPLES AND PRACTICE

Edited by
Ian Davies

CONTINUUM
London and New York

Continuum

Wellington House
125 Strand
London WC2R 0BB

370 Lexington Avenue
New York
NY 10017-6550

First published 2000

British Library Cataloguing-in-Publication Data
A catalogue record for this book is available from the British Library.

ISBN   0 8264 48518 (paperback)
        0 8264 47899 (hardback)

Typeset by BookEns Limited, Royston, Herts.
Printed and bound in Great Britain by Bookcraft (Bath) Ltd

Contents

List of Contributors   vii

Foreword by *John K. Roth, Claremont McKenna College, California*   xi

Introduction: The Challenges of Teaching and Learning about the Holocaust   1
Ian Davies

Part 1 Understanding the Holocaust   9

1 The Roots of Antisemitism   11
Sarah Rees Jones

2 The Jewish Background and the Religious Dimension   25
Sue Foster and Carrie Mercier

3 The Holocaust: Some Reflections and Issues   37
Ian Gregory

4 Teaching about the Holocaust: Perplexities, Issues and Suggestions   49
Ian Gregory

Part 2 International Overviews   61

5 Teaching the Holocaust in Germany   63
Hanns-Fred Rathenow

6 The Education Centre at the Auschwitz-Birkenau Memorial and Museum   77
Krystyna Oleksy

7 Teaching the Holocaust in the United States   93
Samuel Totten

8 Teaching the Holocaust in England   105
Susan Hector

Part 3 Case Studies of Teaching and Learning about the Holocaust   117

9 Teaching the Holocaust through English   119
Nicholas McGuinn

10 **Teaching the Holocaust through History**   135
     Terry Haydn

11 **Teaching the Holocaust through Religious Education**   151
     Sue Foster and Carrie Mercier

12 **Teaching the Holocaust through an Educational Exhibition**   163
     Ian Davies, Ian Gregory and Andrew Lund

Index   175

List of Contributors

Dr Ian Davies is a Senior Lecturer in the Department of Educational Studies at the University of York. His previous experience includes ten years as a teacher in comprehensive schools in England. At York he is responsible for the History initial teacher education course and he supervises graduate research. Publications include *Developing European Citizens* (co-edited with Dr Andreas Sobisch, Sheffield Hallam University Press, 1997) and *Using Documents* (co-written with Chris Webb, English Heritage, 1996).

Sue Foster has since 1997 held a joint appointment as Religious Education Adviser for the City of York and York Diocese. Prior to this she had twenty years' teaching experience in religious education and humanities in comprehensive schools in a number of local education authorities in England. In her present post she supports and advises on religious education, collective worship and equal opportunities in almost 200 schools in the region. She was instrumental in organizing York's hosting of the Anne Frank exhibition in January 1998.

Ian Gregory teaches in the Department of Educational Studies, University of York. His interests are in philosophy and law, particularly as they bear upon educational theory and practice. He is joint author, with Shirley C. Riley, of *Good Citizenship and Educational Provision* (Falmer Press, 1999).

Terry Haydn is lecturer in education at the University of East Anglia and Director of the Secondary Teacher Education Course. He was previously a lecturer in the Department of History, Humanities and Philosophy at the Institute of Education, University of London. For several years he was head of humanities at an inner city comprehensive school in Manchester. His research interests are in the history curriculum and the use of information and communications technology in education.

Susan Hector taught history, social studies and religious education in South London secondary schools for sixteen years before moving into higher education. As senior lecturer in religious education and Holocaust studies at Westminster College, Oxford, she is engaged in the training of teachers at undergraduate and postgraduate levels as well as teaching Judaism to undergraduate students of theology. At the invitation of the Open Society Fund, she delivered a two-week Holocaust course for Lithuanian history teachers at the pedagogical university in Vilnius in 1995. She has given papers at international conferences on Holocaust education and has published articles on teaching the Holocaust in teachers' journals.

Andrew Lund has been teaching history and humanities since 1986, latterly as head of department at Lowfield School, York, before moving to a deputy headship at Garstang High School, Lancashire. Together with colleagues at Lowfield he wrote the history resources which were used by teachers visiting the Anne Frank Educational Trust exhibition during its visit to York in 1998.

Dr Nicholas McGuinn taught in English secondary schools for fourteen years. From 1990 to 1991, he was the Professional Officer for English with the National Curriculum Council. He lectured in education at the University of Hull from 1991 to 1996 and is currently a lecturer in educational studies at the University of York, with particular responsibility for secondary English teaching.

Carrie Mercier is senior lecturer in religious studies at Ripon and York College and is Centre Tutor at the National Society York Religious Education Centre. Previously lecturer in religious education at Westminster College, Oxford, she has taught religious education in both the primary and secondary sectors in schools in the UK. She has also spent some time working in schools in the USA. Her MPhil research area was racism and religious education. She is now involved in initial teacher training and is looking at the issues related to trainee teachers approaching religious education in their school experience.

Krystyna Oleksy graduated in Polish literature and language from Jagiellonian University, Cracow, Poland, where her postgraduate work focused on museum studies. She became senior curator at the State Museum Auschwitz-Birkenau and in 1990 was appointed as the deputy director of the museum; she is also in charge of its Education Department. She is the author of 'Testimonies by Sonderkommando members' (*Terezińskie Studia i Dokumenty*, 1994), 'Changes in the post-camp grounds at Auschwitz' (*Loccumes Protokolle*, 1996), 'Fifty years of the State Museum Auschwitz-Birkenau' (*TONO Bulletin*, 32), 'Poetry created in KL Auschwitz: preface to anthology' and 'A world from the photographs' (*Pro Memoria Bulletin*, 8).

Hanns-Fred Rathenow was born in 1943 in Berlin. He is currently Professor of Education at the Institute for Didactics, Technical University of Berlin. In 1983 he was a visiting professor at the Richardson Institute for Peace and Conflict Research, Lancaster University, and in 1989 he was a visiting fellow at the Centre for Global Education, University of York. He has edited a number of books and has written articles on global education, human rights education and Holocaust education. He is co-editor of the CD-ROM project *Learning from History: National Socialism and the Holocaust in German Education*.

Dr Sarah Rees Jones is a lecturer in medieval history at the University of York, where she teaches on the undergraduate history programme and in the graduate Centre for Medieval Studies. Her main field of research is in medieval urban history. Her publications include a study of the medieval Jewish cemetery in York in J.M. Lilley *et al.* (eds) *The Jewish Burial Ground at Jewbury* (Council for British Archaeology, 1994).

Dr John K. Roth is the Russell K. Pitzer Professor of Philosophy at Claremont McKenna College, where he has taught since 1966. He has published many works on the Holocaust, including books such as *Approaches to Auschwitz: the Holocaust and Its Legacy* (with Richard L. Rubenstein), *Different Voices: Women and the Holocaust* (with Carol Rittner), and, most recently, *Ethics after the Holocaust*. In 1988 Roth was named U.S. National Professor of the Year by the Council for Advancement and Support of Education (CASE) and the Carnegie Foundation for the Advancement of Teaching.

Dr Samuel Totten is a Professor of Curriculum and Instruction at the University of Arkansas, Fayetteville. In his work as an educational consultant with the United States Holocaust Memorial Museum, he co-authored its *Guidelines for Teaching about the Holocaust* (USHMM, 1993). He is also the co-editor of *Teaching the Holocaust* (Allyn and Bacon, 2000) and *Teaching Holocaust Literature* (Allyn and Bacon, 2000).

Foreword

> Taking strange roads ... the ancient procession ... ended in the crematorium.
> (André Schwarz-Bart, *The Last of the Just*)

There was a time when nobody thought about Auschwitz. There was a time when none of the contributors to this volume – or their readers – imagined that it would be critical to study the Holocaust. Once there was no need for this book, but those days are gone. The twentieth century's strange roads show that people will not be equipped to live well in the twenty-first century unless teaching and learning pay attention to the dimensions, principles and practice of Holocaust education. Sensibly and sensitively, this book's insightful and creative essays take significant steps to meet that immense need, which is defined by the fact that human slaughter – particularly as seen in Nazi Germany's attempt to destroy European Jewry – has ravaged history. Without education that is properly focused on those realities, better times remain improbable.

Better times depend on better people. Specifically, better times depend on people who are just. Such persons neither appear by accident nor do they exist abstractly. Instead they live in particular times and places where they have been taught, have learned and practised what justice truly means. Taking those factors into account, editor Ian Davies recalls a local initiative that brought an exhibit about Anne Frank to York in 1998. One thing led to another: stimulated by the Anne Frank exhibit, Holocaust education promoted in York resulted in this book, which has been designed to expand cogent pedagogy that can produce sound teaching and learning in school locales far beyond its origins.

Sarah Rees Jones's opening chapter perceptively underscores that the origins of the essays published here can be traced to York in more ways than one. Late in the twelfth century, for example, what André Schwartz-Bart, a French Jew of Polish descent, called 'the ancient procession' of anti-Jewish violence took its toll on York's Jews. Centuries later, Schwartz-Bart's parents were gassed by the Nazis, but he found his way into the Resistance, escaped after arrest to battle the Nazis again and then continued to resist anti-Semitism and genocide by becoming a post-war writer. His best known work, *The Last of the Just* (1959), a significant early example of Holocaust-related fiction, begins with York's Jews under siege by murderous Christian wrath because they have refused conversion. Trapped in a tower, possessing but a single weapon, they resist by dying willingly at the hand of their leader, Rabbi Yom Tov Levy, who is the last to die when he plunges the dagger into his own throat.

Jewish tradition contains different versions of the legend that informs *The Last of the Just*. Each version suggests, however, that the world's continued existence depends on genuinely righteous persons. For their sake, God withholds destructive wrath, and the rest of humankind is reprieved. In some accounts, there must be 36 who are just; in others, even one *Lamed-Vovnik* is enough. In Schwartz-Bart's adaptation of the *Lamed-Vovnik* tradition, the novel's narrator indicates that another legend emerged in the wake of York's medieval anti-Jewish violence: Rabbi Levy's youngest son survived, and then in a dream he learned that his father's action had moved God. Starting with the rabbi's surviving son, there would be one *Lamed-Vovnik* in every generation of the Levy family.

In Schwartz-Bart's novel, time's passage obscures the *Lamed-Vovnik*'s identity in the Levy line. Nevertheless, Ernie Levy embodies it in the twentieth century. He does so, in particular, when he accompanies Jewish children and tries to comfort them as a German railroad transport deports them from France to their death in the Holocaust's gas chambers. The novel ends in Auschwitz. As Schwartz-Bart's title suggests, Ernie may be the last of the just.

What would it mean if Ernie Levy, or someone like him, were really the last of the just – not only the last in the Levy line but the last of the just: period? It might mean that Jewish legend is false: the world's existence does not depend on just people and maybe not on God either. Or, alternatively, perhaps the question misses the point: Ernie Levy was *not* the last. Just people can still be found; otherwise, the world would be gone. Yet another possibility might be that the world, or at least *a* world, *did* come to an end when the Holocaust decimated Ernie, the children under his care and their people. Perhaps all three of those options, and more, contain grains of truth. Schwartz-Bart leaves such issues open. They invite reflection about Holocaust education that so appropriately fills this book's pages.

The crucial conclusion of Schwartz-Bart's novel is that no-one – neither Ernie Levy nor anyone else – ought to be the last of the just. To the contrary, work must be done to increase the company of the just or the world is indeed imperilled. Essayist Susan Hector echoes her version of that conviction when she sums up the governing theme with which *Teaching the Holocaust* resounds again and again: Holocaust education must emphasize learning *about* and *from* the

Holocaust. This book shows how skilled and dedicated educators –
they work internationally as well as locally – put that principle into
practice through the history they teach, the religious and philosophical questions they raise and the ethical insights they inspire. Their
approaches to teaching about and learning from the antecedents,
realities and implications of the Holocaust, illustrate how Holocaust
education, directed especially toward young students, can help to
nurture the better people, the just men and women, who are required
to curb the ancient procession's ever-present capacity to consign
justice and life itself to the crematorium's flames.

These writers' approaches emphasize that the Holocaust was not
inevitable. Nor are any events related to it. The Holocaust emerged
from decisions and institutions made by human beings who were
responsible for their actions, and who could have acted differently.
Well designed to facilitate learning about and from the Holocaust,
this book rightly fosters responsibility to encourage one another to be
the just persons who can make better times.

John K. Roth
Russell K. Pitzer Professor of Philosophy
Claremont McKenna College, California

Introduction: The Challenges of Teaching and Learning about the Holocaust

Ian Davies

This book aims to:

- promote an awareness of the importance of the need to teach for the reduction of prejudice and discrimination
- develop our understanding of teaching and learning about the Holocaust
- discuss possible ways forward in the challenging area of Holocaust education.

The origins of the book are associated with a visit to York in 1998 of the Anne Frank Educational Trust's exhibition, *Anne Frank: A History for Today*, with liaison and management by the City of York Local Education Authority (LEA). That very successful visit was evaluated. One of the recommendations made by the evaluators, which it was hoped would take further the educational work that had been promoted, was to bring the good work that had been done to the attention of others by means of producing a book. The aim was not only to develop still further our local understandings of the very challenging issues, but also, through our own work and by involving experts from other areas within England and overseas, to bring matters to the attention of others. The discussions that have taken place between the contributors to this book both face to face and electronically have allowed for the development of a text which aims to show diversity of thinking and practice and also a common commitment to the promotion of the need to teach and learn more knowledgeably and sensitively.

This introductory chapter provides a brief overview of some of the issues relating to the way in which the Holocaust can be taught and learned about. The intention is to relate the key issues to the chapters in this book, which is divided into three parts. Part 1, entitled 'Understanding the Holocaust', examines the roots of antisemitism (Sarah Rees Jones) and the nature of Judaism (Sue Foster and Carrie Mercier) and then in two chapters Ian Gregory discusses the perplexities of the Holocaust and examines some pedagogical issues. Part 2 of the book provides international overviews of how the Holocaust is taught in a number of contexts. Three of the chapters are based on individual countries. Germany is discussed by Hanns-Fred Rathenow, the United States by Samuel Totten and England by Susan Hector. The remaining overview was written in Poland by Krystyna Oleksy and is based on Auschwitz. Part 3 comprises four chapters that arise from an approach that is more obviously directly related to classroom experience. Three chapters are subject based. Nicholas McGuinn (English), Terry Haydn (history) and Sue Foster and Carrie Mercier (religious education) discuss the issues and approaches that are relevant to subject teachers. Finally, together with Ian Gregory and Andrew Lund, I discuss the possibility of teaching and learning by means of an educational exhibition.

In the remaining part of this introduction these areas, themes and issues are briefly discussed in three main sections: an outline of the difficulties associated with contextualizing and characterizing the Holocaust, a discussion of some pedagogical challenges, and a more positive final section which attempts to raise for further consideration some possible ways forward.

CONTEXTUALIZING AND CHARACTERIZING THE HOLOCAUST

Three overlapping complexities are mentioned here: the intellectual, the representational and the societal. The use of the phrase 'intellectual complexities' is a rather inadequate means of referring to the potentially unknowable nature of the Holocaust. The roots of antisemitism are examined in Chapter 1 by Rees Jones, and the nature of Judaism in Chapter 2 by Foster and Mercier. In Chapters 3 and 4 Gregory looks at the fundamental issues associated with understanding the Holocaust and how it can be taught. The fact that so many terrible things were done so systematically by so many 'ordinary' people (Browning, 1992) can perhaps never be truly grasped. This is perhaps ultimately a failure of the normal moral framework which is used to deal with our everyday lives and does not necessarily mean that we cannot begin to make *some* sense of the issues. Intellectual approaches to the Holocaust are certainly not all that is required. It is to be hoped that we are more human than simply to play academic games with such terrible events. And yet, to argue that we can only fail in our attempts to deal in some way intellectually with the Holocaust would be simply inaccurate and morally disastrous. We can think clearly and carefully and as such prepare ourselves to do more than shrug our shoulders at the plight of the human condition. This is no simple interjection against modernists or postmodernists (Bauman, 1989; O'Kane, 1997; Milchman and Rosenberg, 1998) but the issues that are raised in those debates do need to be grasped. The unique events of the Holocaust have universal significance. It is in those debates that overwhelmingly important issues emerge more immediately than with any other issue. Those debates show the need to identify a substantive universal moral framework. Within that framework there is space for propositional writing and thinking which does not pretend that a complete moral theory has yet been developed nor that there is a simple guide available for what to do in difficult situations.

Related to the above is the need to consider the ways in which appropriate representation of these issues is made (Braun, 1994). An increasing number of fictional portrayals have been made in the form of novels (Michaels, 1997; Schlink, 1998) and film (Karpf, 1999) either in fictional or semi-fictional form. At a time when the survivors are disappearing, there seems to be a flood of material which at its best ensures that the Holocaust is remembered properly and at its worst misrepresents tragic events and issues for other purposes. Debates about the correct use of key words are valuable. It is not useful to become so embroiled in semantic debates that the study of the past and its connection with contemporary issues is lost, but it is unacceptable if significant groups are not given respect by the use, for example of the word 'gypsy' as opposed to Gypsy or Roma or Sinti. The use of the word 'genocide' to describe conflicts in contemporary Europe and elsewhere is, at the very least, potentially problematic.

The whole notion of how the Holocaust can and should be remembered is a problem. The controversy over the visit by President Reagan to Bitburg in 1985 to remember *all* German war dead is still viewed with discomfort by many (Hartman, 1986). The recent arguments over memorials for the victims of the Holocaust in Berlin are significant. The fact that 9 November is now often remembered in Germany in memory of the fall of the Berlin Wall rather than as Kristallnacht, which took place on that date in 1938, is controversial. Perhaps most important of all there is a fundamental difficulty in knowing how to relate the Holocaust as a unique event which has universal significance if it leads to its use as a 'mere' tool to combat current prejudice and discrimination (see Kinloch, 1998).

The third context discussed here is the societal. There is appalling evidence of a contemporary climate which is hostile to democratic processes. The Council of Europe (1996) has drawn attention to this context and at least one recent international survey of the views of young people supports that view (de Laine, 1997). We must beware of simple formulas and we must realize the extent of the task in creating a decent society. The Holocaust is not simply another branch of academic history, it is not simply unique, it is not simply a warning with clear messages about how to act in all difficult situations. But it can be something about which we attempt clear thought and in relation to which there are some social and political and moral goals which decent people can agree.

PEDAGOGICAL CHALLENGES

Given the difficulties referred to above it is unsurprising that there are massive pedagogical challenges. Perhaps most worrying is that there is some recent evidence that unacceptable views are to be found even among some of those involved in initial teacher education (Wilkins, 1999). It is to be hoped that this disturbing evidence is limited to a small minority of student teachers and teachers. Writers from various countries including those contributing to this book, such as Germany (Rathenow), the USA (Totten) and England (Hector), have noticed the profound difficulties facing teachers. There are other, more general difficulties which have been discussed by a number of writers (Short, 1995; Brown and Davies, 1998). Normally, there is little time devoted to the study of the Holocaust. The work that is done in schools in England takes place in the relatively low status departments of religious education (RE) and history. There is at times little collaboration between those teachers. Some history teachers, for example, aim to teach the Holocaust in only two or three 50 minute lessons to Year 9 pupils (aged 13–14) and many school text books give only a very brief account of the Holocaust.

Another potential pedagogical difficulty is that the Holocaust may be perceived by at least some teachers as a rather distant event which is used 'merely' as an example in their efforts to teach for tolerance. Some teachers have seen a wide range of topics being suitable for this purpose, including the actions by William the Conqueror following the invasion of 1066, the massacre at Drogheda by Cromwell, the clearing of the Scottish highlands, slavery, living conditions in the nineteenth century, the Vietnam war and the wars in Rwanda and the Balkans (Brown and Davies, 1998). In such circumstances the motivation to teach the Holocaust may be weakened.

Perhaps the most difficult of the pedagogical issues relates to the choice that teachers have to make in deciding how to present the Holocaust and what sort of educational aims are valid. There are many points wrapped within what could be generally described as the difficulty of placing the Holocaust appropriately on some sort of affective–cognitive continuum. Teachers rightly do not want to see the Holocaust only in intellectual or academic terms, and yet emotion is in itself not enough. There has to be clear rational thought as well as an emotional response. Even if teachers are engaging with the complex questions and issues surrounding the Holocaust, the climate that affects schools makes it very challenging to discuss powerful issues appropriately. The use of micro-historical studies in school teaching in an attempt to make the events and issues more understandable and which is a reflection of academic developments (Browning, 1992; Goldhagen, 1996) probably puts these difficulties into sharper relief. Young people do need to know about the horror of the Holocaust but what form should that take and at what sort of responses should teachers aim?

SOME POSITIVE WAYS FORWARD?

The previous sections should not be read pessimistically. There is a pressing need to teach and learn about the Holocaust and there are a number of positive ways forward. There is no intention that this book should provide simple answers for huge difficulties and, of course, there must be space for different approaches. But, optimistically, teachers do see this work as important; there are excellent books for teachers and children (Richter, 1987; Supple, 1992; Landau, 1998) and resources and other services including research are supplied by various organizations and centres including those mentioned in the chapters in this book.

Teachers still have flexibility in what they decide to do and by maintaining a proper professional independence there is much valuable work that can take place. McGuinn (Chapter 9) argues that they should always be careful to exert the vigilance necessary to sustain democratic accountability. Their engagement with the process of school reform and their selection and interpretation of the forms of knowledge that are used with young people are a vital part of any country's commitment to the promotion of a decent society.

Part of what teachers can do is to ensure that as far as possible the fundamental aspects of what happened during the Holocaust are shown accurately. The three most commonly related subjects for teaching about the Holocaust are history, English and religious education. In Part 3 Haydn, McGuinn and Foster and Mercier provide ideas on which teachers can work. By emphasizing accurate knowledge, the skills of critical analysis, the development of awareness of the manipulation of language, and the portrayal of religious and moral issues in a sensitive and living manner, these subjects have much to offer. Also positive ways forward can be found in the use of cross-curricular efforts; an example is given in Chapter 12 in the discussion of the exhibition by the Anne Frank Educational Trust by myself, Gregory and Lund.

There are many huge and varied challenges associated with teaching and learning about the Holocaust. Intellectually and pedagogically there are huge obstacles to overcome. It would be naive to suggest that this book does any more than to highlight those issues. But it is to be hoped that there are also enough positive ways forward to give further encouragement to teachers and others to be bold enough to press ahead.

ACKNOWLEDGEMENTS

This project would not have started without the good work of Michael Peters who as Director of Educational Services, City of York made possible the visit of the Anne Frank Educational Trust's exhibition to York. Gillian Walnes of the Anne Frank Educational Trust was always extremely helpful. The authors wish to thank members of staff at the Holocaust Educational Trust for their very supportive work. The people of York within the museum education service and beyond who made the visit of the exhibition so successful in their role as teachers, guides, other helpers or as visitors to the exhibition deserve our thanks. Particular mention can be made of Lynn Allerton, Ruth Dass, Jocelyn Hayes, Val Kinser, Andrew

Lovett, Liz Shiels, Ben Sugar, Claire Suttill and Yvonne Weir. Dr Gillian Klein was a source of great assistance when the initial plans for the book were being made and gave a number of valuable suggestions about the writing of the material. Chapter 12 appeared in Volume 17, no. 3, pp. 43–8 (Summer 1999) of the journal *Multicultural Teaching*. Rabbi Douglas Charing commented in a very helpful way on the chapters by Sue Foster and Carrie Mercier. Chris Brown made a helpful contribution to Chapter 5. For the work described in Chapter 8, Susan Hector wishes to thank the teachers of history and religious education at Aylesbury High School; Beaconsfield School; Bishop Stopford C of E School, Kettering; Blessed George Napier RC School, Banbury; Burford School and Community College; Churchfields School and Ridgeway School, Swindon; Didcot Girls' School; Faringdon School; Gosford Hill School, Kidlington; John Mason School, Abingdon; King Alfred's School, Wantage; Lodge Park School, Corby; Lord William's School, Thame; Matthew Arnold School, Oxford; Misbourne School, Great Missenden; Ousedale School, Newport Pagnell; Portsmouth Grammar School; Royal Grammar School, High Wycombe; St Birinus School, Didcot; Wallingford School; Wootton Upper School, Bedfordshire; and especially Deborah Stevenson, the religious education department and pupils in Year 9 at Wood Green School, Witney. I am sure that the list of names above is incomplete. I hope that the other people who made a very helpful contribution to this book will forgive the omissions.

REFERENCES

Bauman, Z. (1989) *Modernity and the Holocaust*. Cambridge: Polity Press.

Bowker, J. (ed.) (1991) *Secondary Media Education: A Curriculum Statement*. London: British Film Institute.

Braun, R. (1994) The Holocaust and problems of historical representation, *History and Theory*, **33** 172–97.

Brown, M. and Davies, I. (1998) The Holocaust and education for citizenship: the teaching of history, religion and human rights in England, *Educational Review*, **50**(1), 75–83.

Browning, C.L. (1992) *Ordinary Men: Reserve Police Battalion 101 and the Final Solution in Poland*. New York, HarperCollins.

Council of Europe (1996) *History Teaching and the Promotion of Democratic Values and Tolerance: A Handbook for Teachers*. Strasbourg: Council of Europe.

De Laine, M. (1997) Third of teenagers deny Holocaust, *Times Educational Supplement*, 4 July.

Goldhagen, D. (1996) *Hitler's Willing Executioners: Ordinary Germans and the Holocaust*. London: Little, Brown.

Hartman, G. (ed.) (1986) *Bitburg in Moral and Political Perspective.* Bloomington: Indiana University Press.

Karpf, A. (1998) Let's pretend life is beautiful, *Guardian*, 3 April.

Kinloch, N. (1998) Learning about the Holocaust: moral or historical question? *Teaching History*, **93**, 44–6.

Landau, R. (1998) *Studying the Holocaust: Issues, Readings and Documents.* London: Routledge.

Michaels, A. (1997) *Fugitive Pieces.* London: Bloomsbury.

Milchman, A. and Rosenberg, A. (eds) (1998) *Postmodernism and the Holocaust.* Amsterdam: Rodopi.

O'Kane, R.H.T. (1997) Modernity, the Holocaust and politics, *Economy and Society*, **26**(1), 43–61.

Richter, H.P. (1987) *Friedrich.* London: Puffin.

Schlink, B. (1998) *The Reader.* London: Phoenix.

Short, G. (1995) The Holocaust in the National Curriculum: a survey of teachers' attitudes and practices, *Journal of Holocaust Education*, **4**, 167–88.

Supple, C. (1992) *From Prejudice to Genocide: Learning about the Holocaust.* Stoke-on-Trent: Trentham Books.

Wilkins, C. (1999) Making 'Good Citizens': the social and political attitudes of PGCE students, *Oxford Review of Education,* **25**(1 and 2), 217–30.

Part 1

Understanding the Holocaust

Chapter 1

The Roots of Antisemitism

Sarah Rees Jones

Josce set the first example by cutting the throats of his wife, Anna, and of his sons. The terrible responsibility for killing the women and children then seems to have fallen to the fathers of each Jewish household in turn. The latter probably met their own fate by the knife of Rabbi Yomtob, who appears to have ended the slaughter by taking Josce's life just before his own ... At daybreak the following morning the 'wretched remnants of the Jews' appealed for mercy in return for Christian baptism; but as they left the castle under a calculatedly insincere promise of clemency, the 'cruel butchers' who followed Richard Malebisse and the other leaders of the pogrom massacred them all. (Dobson, 1974, pp. 27–8)

The massacre of the Jews of York, on 16 March 1190, is a permanent reminder that the kind of violence suffered by Jews during the Holocaust has a long history. Students need to understand this history in order to understand not only what happened in the Holocaust, but also why it happened. There can be no simple answers – not least because anyone who considers Jewish history now, whether Jew or Gentile, cannot escape the consequences of the Holocaust themselves. It is difficult to discuss such an emotive subject rationally. Reason seems a cold instrument with which to measure pain, and indeed much of the history of antisemitism is beyond reason. However, to dismiss antisemitism as a 'fantasy of diseased minds' also runs the risk of minimizing the degree to which it was in fact normalized within the legal framework and culture of western European states (Langmuir, 1990; Lindemann, 1997).

Historians of the Holocaust are also divided as to how far back the origins of antisemitism should be traced (Katz, 1980; Lindemann, 1997). Some argue that the Holocaust was a uniquely modern event, the product of modern science, modern media and modern politics, which created new forms of popular antisemitism after the 1870s. This chapter takes a different perspective. Legal and popular discrimination against Jews has a history which stretches back over fifteen centuries before the dawn of the nineteenth century. Anti-Semitism was not a product of a single time, place or people, but played a profound role in the foundation of western society.

So we need to explore the history of antisemitism, yet in doing so we need to avoid promoting the idea that antisemitism is inevitable; that Jews only suffer and that Christians only persecute. For this reason many modern Jewish historians have rejected such *Leidens-geschichte* (suffering history) in favour of a more wide-ranging treatment of Jewish history (Baron, 1952). Their rejection of a history which focuses only on the suffering of Jews in part reflects a modern, secularized rejection of Jewish religious traditions in which suffering was seen as God's punishment for the collective sin of the community, and central to the community's relationship with God. This in turn raises one of the most sensitive questions. How far were Jews themselves responsible for antisemitism? Did the Jewish religion encourage a culture of 'self-blame' which only made Jews more contemptible in the eyes of their persecutors? Did the bitter arguments between modernized and traditional Jew in the nineteenth century contribute to the rhetoric of modern antisemitism, increasing the danger for those who would, or could, not 'assimilate'? Did Jews believe that they were superior to Christians; was the fear and contempt mutual, and mutually isolating?

If the Holocaust had not happened, if violent massacres of Jews had indeed been confined to the Middle Ages, then perhaps these questions would not seem as sensitive as they do at the present time. Instead, our sensitivity towards the past has been reawakened by the Holocaust; in turn, we need to understand that past in order to understand both the Holocaust itself and the continuing legacy of antisemitism in modern society.

This short chapter can provide only the briefest of overviews of the origins of antisemitism, and inevitably much detail and many issues will be omitted. The focus of the chapter is also, primarily, on northern Europe. It was between the tenth and the fifteenth centuries that Judaism took root in the north, and it was in the same period that the foundations of modern antisemitism were laid in the laws of newly emerging states and in popular culture. In order to understand this critical medieval history, however, we need to go back still further to the establishment of the Christian religion in the Roman empire.

THE ORIGINS OF JEWISH COMMUNITIES IN EUROPE

Exile and persecution are, indeed, prominent themes in Jewish history, recalled every year in the ritual of the Pesach (Passover). The first Jewish Diaspora (the dispersion of the Jews from their homeland) began with the exile of Jews in Egypt and Babylon in the eighth and sixth centuries BCE, and continued in the Hellenistic and Roman periods in the voluntary migration of Jews as soldiers, merchants and bureaucrats. Conversions also significantly increased the size and dispersal of Judaism, which, in this period, was an evangelizing faith. By the first century CE up to 10 per cent of the population of the Roman empire was Jewish (Stow, 1992). The largest communities were in the central and eastern Mediterranean, but there were also small groups of Jews in northern cities such as Cologne and Paris (Beinart, 1992). As these communities flourished, so they gained privileges and full legal recognition under Roman law.

The destruction of the Temple in Jerusalem in 70, at the command of the Emperor Titus, and the final dissolution of the Jewish province of Judaea in 135 by Hadrian, were definitive events in the Diaspora and, gradually, Imperial attitudes towards Jewish communities also began to change. In 202 all proselytizing activities, by both Jews and Christians, were outlawed, but, after the Emperor Constantine ended the persecution of Christians in 313, such restrictions increasingly applied to the Jews alone.

CHRISTIAN AND JEW IN THE ROMAN EMPIRE

Christianity began as a Jewish sect, and was only gradually recognized as a distinct religion. Yet the very nature of Christianity, at least from the time of Paul, also forced Christians to challenge the beliefs of Jews who did not accept Christ as Messiah (Parkes, 1934; Edwards, 1988; Stow, 1992). The new followers of Christ thus inflamed divisions among competing Jewish sects, which in part fuelled the Jewish revolts suppressed by Nero and Hadrian. Increasing animosity between Christian and non-Christian Jew was in turn heightened by stricter imperial religious laws, under which, initially, Christians were singled out by their greater persecution. This antagonism was, at times, associated with a vitriolic polemic between the leaders of both religions. According to some rabbinic sources, for example, Christ was a magician in partnership with Satan; he was the bastard son of a whore and his followers, the 'sectaries', were worse even than the pagans. The very presence of Christians, some argued, threatened the Jews' salvation (Stow, 1992).

Despite persecution from both Imperial and some Jewish authorities, Christianity continued to grow among both Jews and, most rapidly, Gentiles. The reasons for the diffusion of Christianity, in the first two centuries after Christ, remain a mystery (Lane Fox, 1988; Fletcher, 1997). At first it spread slowly, taking root in the cities – Alexandria, Ephesus, Carthage, Rome – where communities of Jews already flourished. By the third century the new religion was attracting converts of higher status, and, following the adoption of the faith by the Emperor Constantine, Christianity was slowly transformed into the established religion of the imperial state.

Emperors after Constantine increasingly developed a theory of monarchy which emphasized the power of the ruler over both spiritual and secular affairs (Fletcher, 1997). Their patronage of Christianity thus increasingly led them to assert that religion over all others, and by the time of Justinian (483–565), an attack on the Church was considered the gravest of assaults on the Emperor himself. The fourth to sixth centuries were therefore critical in laying the foundations of later relations between Christian and Jew. In essence two contrasting attitudes emerged.

First, there was imperial law. Two great collections of Roman law, the Theodosian Code (*c*. 430) and the Justinian Code (*c*. 500), established a framework for the state regulation of Jews which was to persist throughout the Middle Ages and into the modern period, in the civil law traditions of European states (Parkes, 1934; Edwards, 1988; Katz, 1980). The Theodosian Code represented a balance between protecting basic Jewish rights, and ensuring that the dominant religion, Christianity, was not 'contaminated' by Jewish influences. The Justinian Code was more extreme. It abolished the legal status of the Jewish religion and curtailed the economic and legal activities of Jews. In both laws Jews were forbidden to proselytize, to own Christian slaves, to sit in judgement over Christians (for example by holding public office in the imperial courts) or to build synagogues without licence. The Jewish scripture (the Torah) was not to be read in public, and Jews were not to ridicule the Christian faith. On the other hand, violent attacks by Christians on Jewish rituals, synagogues and the Sabbath were also forbidden, and the forcible conversion, physical segregation or expulsion of Jews were not supported by the law (Parkes, 1934; Stow, 1992). The less severe Theodosian Code had the greater influence in western Europe, especially in the laws developed by the western papacy. Although these laws did not permit Jews an equal place in imperial society, they did seek to provide for the continuation of the Jewish way of life. Increasingly, however, they made the toleration of Jewish life dependent on the will of the monarch and the freedoms that he was prepared to extend within his jurisdiction. Although the motivation behind the law was the further separation and distinction of the Christian and Jewish religions, the means through which this was achieved were by the regulation, and to some extent segregation, of social and economic activities. Theologically based anti-Judaism was to be imposed through the increasing control of the daily lives of the Jews as a distinct people. An important distinction had thus been blurred. Anti-Judaism, or the criticism of a religion on theological grounds, had acquired the potential to develop into antisemitism, the persecution of a people, through the regulation of daily life by the state on the pretext of religious purity.

Although imperial laws envisaged a continued Jewish presence in Christian society, the fourth to sixth centuries also saw the development of other, more violent, attitudes toward the Jews which were considerably less tolerant of their continued existence within a Christian state. In some cities the substantial presence of wealthy and powerful Jewish families was seen as a threat to Christian rule, and the constant intermingling of Jewish and Christian populations was deemed a hazard to Christian salvation. Christians were in some respects as much the target of these concerns as Jews, for the real fear of local episcopal authorities was that the two religions were still entangled in the rituals and minds of the laity; indeed, that Jews continued to convert Christians to their faith. In some places Christians and Jews still worshipped at the same shrines, venerated the same relics and used the same prayers and psalms (Ginzberg, 1996). In the city of Antioch, for example, both groups shared a veneration for the Maccabees (Jewish 'freedom fighters' of the second century BCE), but in 380 the synagogue where they were believed to be buried was forcibly seized and turned into a church. A few years later the bishop of Antioch, John Chrysostum, wrote about the Jews as the 'arch-symbol of evil'. His language recalled the vitriolic abuse of earlier conflicts: Jews were 'ruled by gluttony and licentiousness', 'their souls are the dwelling place of demons' and, most sinisterly, Jews were like those animals, who when they 'are unfit for work, are marked for slaughter' (Stow, 1992).

Chrysostum's images of degradation were drawn from the

commonplace stock of Roman insults – gluttony, sexual perversion, devil worship and sadism. His incendiary language reflected increasingly violent efforts, in some communities, to enforce the dominance of the Church, which contradicted the limited toleration of the Jewish faith advocated by imperial law. As local Christian authorities defined the Christian faith, and its differences from Judaism, so too they sought to impose clear distinctions between Christian and Jewish peoples, where once those distinctions had been unclear. In Minorca, in 418, the Jewish synagogue was razed to the ground and the entire Jewish population converted to Christianity under the threat of violence. Ginzberg (1992) and others have argued that this was a consequence of deliberate efforts by local bishops to convert the laity to a purer Christianity by forcibly ending Jewish proselytization. Indeed, the concern that the Christian flock would drift away to Judaism was a continued preoccupation of Christian rulers throughout the early Middle Ages in Mediterranean Europe, and was sometimes the pretext for forcible conversion or for anti-Jewish laws. While many converts to Judaism were people of modest means, such as the peasants of the Lyonnais, who converted in the ninth century in order to gain a remission from taxes due to the Jews employed as tax-collectors, others were more prominent, such as Andrew, archbishop of Bari, who became a Jew in *c.* 1066, presumably on theological grounds (Fletcher, 1997). The common scriptural roots of the two religions made each a most dangerous threat to the other.

The ecclesiastical fear of Jewish proselytization was perhaps, ironically, a testimony to the continued influence of Jews who were so integrated in the community that they could barely be distinguished from their 'Christian' neighbours. Nevertheless the danger was always that in the process of separating Christian from Jew, the Jew became the 'Other'. If the Christian was represented as godly, pious and clean, then the Jew, who did not accept the Christian message, could be represented as the antithesis of the Christian: the demonic, impious and unclean.

THE LATER MIDDLE AGES

On the twenty-third of Iyar [18 May 1096] they attacked the [Jewish] community of Worms. The community divided into two groups; some remained in their homes and others fled to the local bishop seeking refuge. Those who remained in their homes were set upon by steppe-wolves [cf. Jeremiah 6] who pillaged men, women and infants, children and old people. They pulled down the stairways and destroyed the houses, looting and plundering; and they took the Torah scroll, trampled it in the mud, and tore and burned it ... Seven days later, on the new moon of Sivan, those Jews who were still in the court of the bishop were subjected to great anguish. The enemy dealt them the same cruelty as the first group and put them to the sword ... The enemy stripped them naked, dragged them along, and then cast them off, sparing only a small number whom they forcibly baptised in their profane waters. The number of those slain during the two days was approximately eight hundred. (*Chronicle of Solomon bar Simson*, cited Fletcher 1997, pp. 317–18)

In 1003 the Islamic ruler of Palestine began a persecution of Christians which culminated in the destruction of the church of the Holy Sepulchre at Jerusalem. Immediately stories began to circulate that this persecution was provoked by Jews (Fletcher, 1997). Organized violence against Jewish communities in western Europe escalated, as preachers advocating a crusade to reconquer Jerusalem also spread the idea that the Jews were plotting the destruction of the Christian community just as, they alleged, Jews had been responsible for the death of Christ. Europe was swept by a wave of violent pogroms (Beinart, 1992; Stow, 1992; Chazan, 1997).

The pogroms of 1096 and after marked a decisive shift in anti-Jewish attitudes in western Europe. Whereas much earlier anti-Jewish activity had focused on converting Jews, or 'Judaized' Christians, to Christianity, the new attacks aimed to eradicate Jewish communities altogether. Whereas earlier fears had focused on the proselytizing activities of Jews, the new terror centred on Jews as the murderous enemies of Christ. Whereas much of the evidence for Jewish-Christian conflict in the early Middle Ages relates to southern Europe, the pogroms associated with the crusading movement began in northern Europe.

Numerous reasons for these changes have been suggested. The Jewish communities of northern Europe were relatively young. Although some northern Roman cities had supported small Jewish communities, the major migration of Jews into northern Europe occurred between the tenth and the twelfth centuries, and they accounted for no more than 2 per cent of the population (Beinart, 1992; Stow, 1992; Chazan, 1997). The Jews of York, for example, had probably been settled for no more than twenty years by the time of the York massacre in 1190 (Dobson, 1974). Furthermore the new communities were often sponsored by rulers who were increasing their own power over their subjects, and Jews were introduced by them to unpopular positions as money-lenders and tax-collectors. The leaders of the York uprising against the Jews were minor local nobility who had become indebted to the Jews and resented their 'protection' by the crown (Dobson, 1974). Whereas the Jews of southern Europe were well integrated in society, the greater violence in the north may thus have been a reaction against the 'imposition' of immigrant communities and their association with unpopular authorities (Chazan, 1997). Thus the real anxieties, underlying Jewish persecution, may have been those of a lay population subject to increasing economic, political and fiscal pressures, for which the Jews were 'scapegoats'. Such explanations would clearly find parallels in the explanation of more modern Jewish persecutions (Lindemann, 1997).

Other explanations for increased anti-Jewish violence are less dependent on drawing parallels with modern antisemitism. Contemporary changes within Christianity, in particular an increased interest in the humanity of Christ, may have been responsible (Stow, 1992; Chazan, 1997). The more realistic art of the later Middle Ages, the increased sympathy for the holy family, especially the Virgin Mary, a growing focus on the sacrament of the Eucharist and an associated interest in the passion of Christ's crucifixion were all typical of the 'humanizing' religion of the later medieval Christian. For Jews, however, these new devotions carried the threat that their relationship with Christians would also be characterized by a greater emphasis on personal suffering and violent death. Representations of Jews as 'Christ-slayers' became more widespread and a new image of the 'murderous Jew' who, in extreme versions of the libel, drank the blood of Christians in a deliberate perversion of the Christian Eucharist, began to circulate. Stories of the ritual abuse and murder of Christian children by Jews, or of Jews poisoning water supplies, became common. When thousands died in the plague of the Black Death of 1347–9, many believed that the 'murderous Jew' was responsible (Beinart, 1992; Horrox, 1994).

The twin roots of the emotive rhetoric of crude antisemitism, contrasted with a more temperate official anti-Judaism, thus remained the stock of medieval attitudes. The crudest forms of antisemitism, in which Jews were represented as obscene or perverse, were most likely to circulate among local élites (Bale, 1998). At times of tension this hatred could inflame violent attacks on the Jews. After the first wave of pogroms associated with crusading fervour, later persecutions included the Reindfleisch and Armledder massacres in hundreds of towns across the Rhineland and northern Germany between 1298 and 1330, the pogroms which swept Europe in the wake of the Black Death, or the mass uprisings against the Jews in Spain in 1391 when 400,000 Jews were either killed or forcibly converted (Beinart, 1992; Chazan, 1997).

By contrast, legal attitude to Jews continued to be conditioned by the constraint of Imperial law, and anti-Judaism, rather than antisemitism, continued to characterize Christian theology. In particular Christian theologians frequently argued that Jews, as the first chosen people of Christ, must be respected; papal bulls and diocesan letters were issued condemning violence against Jews and their property, and urging respect for Jewish religious ceremonies, cemeteries and synagogues, under threat of excommunication. Nevertheless violence remained a reality, and could be the cause of greater segregation between the two communities. The earliest Jewish ghettos – walled cities-within-cities built in some Rhineland towns in the fourteenth century – were sponsored by local bishops to defend the Jews against Christian violence (Beinart, 1992; Stow, 1992).

The ghetto not only protected the Jew against Christian violence, but also protected the Christian against perceived spiritual corruption. The creation of two parallel communities, each with its own customs and officials, only faintly indicated by the concepts of imperial law, became the solution favoured by both ecclesiastical and secular laws of the later Middle Ages. All Christian contacts with Jews should be restricted and supervised. For example, Jews were, from 1215, to wear a distinctive dress or badge, they were not to carry weapons, not to hold public office, not to employ or marry Christians and not to use public bathhouses (which were commonly associated with brothels) at the same time as Christians. Segregation of Jewish communities, whether physically in a ghetto, or, more often, administratively by the law, was the ideal.

This segregation of Jews was often accompanied by pressure to convert. In London a 'house of the converted' was established under royal patronage. In Spain, the activities of the Inquisition in converting Jews and Muslims, and in policing converts, became notorious. Royal patronage, however, only emphasized the dependence of the Jew on the king's will. The ultimate segregation was the exclusion of the Jew from his state altogether. In 1290 Edward I of England became the first king to expel Jews from his kingdom. Financially, the Jewish community was of declining value to the crown (Roth, 1964). Spiritually, the king claimed that the conversion of the Jews had failed, therefore their property was seized and they were expelled from his kingdom (Stow, 1992). Jews were not officially allowed to resettle in England until 1655. The English expulsion was followed by expulsions from France and, most destructively, from Spain in 1492. Expulsions from some parts of Germany continued, with mixed results, throughout the sixteenth century (Edwards, 1988). Of the exiled Jews, many settled initially in Germany and then moved eastward, into central Europe and Russia. Exiles from Spain moved east to Italy, Asia Minor, north Africa and Palestine (Beinart, 1992). For those communities which survived, settlement in a defensible ghetto became an increasingly common way of life, especially after 1555.

THE DIASPORA AND THE JEWISH FAITH

Despite violent persecution, segregation and some increasingly crude antisemitism, Jewish communities continued to flourish in medieval northern Europe, giving rise to a new Jewish identity, that of the Ashkenazi, as opposed to the Sephardic Jews of Mediterranean Europe. Any history of the Jews which focused only on the history of antisemitism would be profoundly misleading. Indeed, the ultimate success of northern European Jewry is indicated by the fact that there are now probably more Jews in the world of Ashkenazic than of Sephardic origin. Jews became deeply integrated at all levels of society, especially in the towns, but also in some rural communities (Baron, 1952; Golb, 1998).

Important Jewish schools were established and new traditions of devotion and scriptural exegesis among the Ashkenazi Jews developed (Stow, 1992; Golb, 1998). Of particular importance was the Hasidic movement, which originated in cities such as Speyer and Regensburg in the twelfth and thirteenth centuries. In common with other northern scholars, the Hasidim sought to adapt the Jewish law, particularly the Talmud (itself largely the product of the Diaspora in fifth century Persia), to the conditions of life in northern Europe in the late Middle Ages (Stow, 1992).

Hasidism was also conditioned by the experience of intense persecution. The Hasidim embraced traditional beliefs that persecution and exile were a punishment for the collective sin of the community, and linked its expiation with the strictest adherence not only to traditional Jewish custom, but increasingly to local Jewish custom. Commentary on the Jewish law became more localized in both content and language, using German (the origins of Yiddish) or French instead of Hebrew. This internal reform of northern Judaism certainly contributed to the increasing distinction of Jew from Christian. Indeed, the Ashkenazi later developed a much greater sense of separation from Christian society than did the Sephardim, who were more fully assimilated (Katz, 1973; Lindemann, 1997). Yet Hasidism also created a new Jewish culture which was as indigenous to northern Europe as any contemporary Christian movement (Stow,

1992). Along with integration into the economic life of northern Europe, the distinctively European devotion of the Hasidim supported the successful diffusion of northern Jewish communities. Perhaps, not surprisingly, the heirs to this tradition in the modern world have included those opposed to the creation of a Jewish state outside Europe. The Hasid was both distinctively Jewish and distinctively European at the same time.

The broad sweep of northern Jewish learning was paralleled, especially in the beginning, by that of Christian philosophers, many of whom used Hebraic scholarship, benefited from Jewish access to Arabic texts of classical authors or discussed shared theological traditions (Stow, 1992; Abulafia, 1995). Common scriptural origins made Jewish scholarship essential to continuing Christian theology. Even in the most remote cities, such as York, the first Jewish settlers may have arrived as scholars sponsored by the province's archbishop (Dobson, 1974). Academic freedom to study the relationship between Christian and Jewish traditions was restrained after 1240, when the Talmud was condemned as heretical by the Pope and publicly burned in Paris. Nevertheless the study of Hebrew, and Christian interest in Kabbalah, a form of Jewish mysticism, continued to keep Jewish learning alive among Christian scholars until the time of Luther and Calvin (Edwards, 1988).

MEDIEVAL TO MODERN

The Enlightenment of the eighteenth century, rather than the Reformation of the sixteenth, is generally regarded as the significant divide between the medieval and modern history of the Jews (Katz, 1973; Edwards, 1988; Lindemann, 1997). Secularization, especially the weakening of ties between church and state, presented fundamental challenges to a society, both Christian and Jewish, whose relations and identity had been traditionally defined in religious terms. The prospect of emancipation from the ghetto, of full integration into citizenship on equal terms with non-Jews, offered new freedoms, but only, many argued, at the expense of assimilation and the loss of a truly Jewish, religious identity. The place of the Jew in modern society was a matter of vigorous debate among Jews, as well as non-Jews.

Secularization also raised new terrors. Persecution conducted according to ideas of 'racial purity' supposedly determined by biological, rather than religious, criteria, was as much the product of modern science as was the technology of transport and murder. Yet the demonizing of the Jew in modern Europe – the murderous, scheming, dirty, overpowerful Jew – built on images established in popular culture centuries before. The engineers of the Holocaust in northern Europe built upon medieval foundations. Legally these foundations borrowed from the law codes of the later Roman empire. Theologically their anti-Judaism was built on the work of Paul and Augustine. Even crude antisemitism used the same emotive rhetoric and obscene images as ancient fears and insults. But it was during the later medieval period new official policies of forcible conversion, arbitrary physical segregation and expulsion were adopted by the fledgling Christian states of Europe, and new institutions, such as the ghetto, were introduced into Jewish life as a consequence. Without these changes, and without the demonization of the Jew which tended to follow in the popular imagination from their outcast status, twentieth-century antisemitism could not have taken the form it did. The long history of antisemitism suggests that it will not easily be uprooted. We still need to consider its subtle legacies, even after the Holocaust.

REFERENCES

Abulafia, A.S. (1995) *Christians and Jews in the Twelfth Century Renaissance*. London: Routledge.

Bale, A. (1998) Holy shit: medieval Christianity and anti-Semitic scatology, unpublished MA dissertation, Medieval Studies, University of York.

Baron, S.W. (1952) *A Social and Religious History of the Jews*, 2nd rev. edn, 18 vols., New York: Columbia University Press.

Beinart, H. (1992) *Atlas of Medieval Jewish History*. New York: Simon and Schuster.

Chazan, R. (1997) *Medieval Stereotypes and Modern Anti-Semitism*. Berkeley, CA: University of California Press.

Dobson, R.B. (1974) *The Jews of Medieval York and the Massacre of March 1190*. Borthwick Papers 45, York: St Anthony's Press.

Edwards, J. (1988) *The Jews in Christian Europe 1400–1700*. London: Routledge.

Fletcher, R. (1997) *The Conversion of Europe from Paganism to Christianity 371–1386 A.D.* London: HarperCollins.

Ginzberg, C. (1996) The conversion of Minorcan Jews (417–418): an experiment in the history of historiography. In S.L. Waught and P. D. Diehl (eds) *Christendom and its Discontents: Exclusion, Persecution and Rebellion 1000–1500*. Cambridge: Cambridge University Press.

Golb, N. (1998) *The Jews in Medieval Normandy: A Social and Intellectual History*. Cambridge: Cambridge University Press.

Horrox, R. (ed.) (1994) *The Black Death*. Manchester Medieval Series. Manchester and New York: Manchester University Press.

Katz, J. (1973) *Out of the Ghetto: The Social Background of Jewish Emancipation 1770–1870*. New York: Harvard University Press, reprinted Schocken Books, 1978.

Katz, J. (1980) *From Prejudice to Destruction: Anti-Semitism 1700–1933*. Cambridge, MA: Harvard University Press.

Lane Fox, R. (1988) *Pagans and Christians in the Mediterranean World from the Second Century AD to the Conversion of Constantine*. Harmondsworth: Penguin.

Langmuir, G.I. (1990) *History, Religion and Anti-Semitism*. London: Tauris.

Lindemann, A.S. (1997) *Esau's Tears: Modern Anti-Semitism and the Rise of the Jews*. Cambridge: Cambridge University Press.

Parkes, J.W. (1934) *The Conflict of the Church and the Synagogue: A Study in the Origins of Anti-Semitism*. London: Soncino Press.

Roth, C. (1964) *A History of the Jews in England*, 3rd edn. Oxford: Clarendon Press.

Stow, K. (1992) *Alienated Minority: The Jews of Medieval Latin Europe*. Cambridge, MA: Harvard University Press.

Chapter 2

The Jewish Background and the Religious Dimension

Sue Foster and Carrie Mercier

It is impossible to tell the story of the Holocaust without talking about 'the Jews'. This chapter begins by considering what students who are learning about the Holocaust might understand by the term 'the Jews' and why this is a relevant matter for their teachers to take into account. The chapter goes on to argue that students who have some background knowledge of the Jewish faith, its beliefs and practices are more likely to have a sympathetic understanding of who the Jews are and are therefore in a better position to understand many of the events of the Holocaust than those who have no such background knowledge. The chapter then considers ways in which teaching on Judaism can contribute to the presentation of the Jewish people in a positive light and thereby help to counter some negative stereotypes. The chapter goes on to ask whether students who are familiar with the beliefs and traditions of the Jewish people are better equipped with the skills for intercultural understanding than those who have not been introduced to the study of religious beliefs different from their own. Holocaust education is not only about the past but also about the future and 'never again' is the thought that many teachers hold on to in their approach to Holocaust studies. It is for this reason that this chapter considers ways in which schools, through the study of Judaism, might promote opportunities for dialogue and co-operation between different cultural and religious groups.

In telling the story of the Holocaust, in history or in social studies or in any other area of the curriculum, the teacher will at some point introduce 'the Jews'. Perhaps, when the Jews are first mentioned, the teacher will ask the students 'And who are the Jews – can anyone tell me?' What sort of answer is the teacher likely to get: 'Aren't they people who pray in a synagogue?' 'Don't they wear skull caps and ringlets?' 'They are the people mentioned in the Bible.' What picture do our students have when they hear the term 'the Jews'? Do they relate the term 'the Jews' to the religion of Judaism at all? Some teachers might argue that we could simply say that the Jews are a group of people with a shared history and culture and leave it at that. We could, but the students we teach will have picked up a variety of messages from the media, their family, friends and peers and it is likely that they will have heard negative comments and stereotypes. It is therefore essential to present the Jewish people in a positive light. Nevertheless, the question 'Who is a Jew?' is not an easy one to answer.

For many Jews, being Jewish is about belonging to a religious community that has a deep sense of its covenant relationship with God. For others, being Jewish has very little to do with being religious. It is about an identity based on many things including a shared history and culture and for some a strong commitment to Israel as a homeland. Nevertheless, even if the religious dimension is no longer a major influence in life for many Jews, the religion of their forebears has played an important part in shaping their identity. In fact, to answer the question 'Who are the Jews?' it is impossible to ignore the religious dimension to the issue. Sacks (1995) in responding to the question of Jewish identity considers the difficulties that arise when defining Judaism without reference to the religious destiny:

> To be a Jew was to be born into a people with a shared history of suffering and hope. But it was also to be born into a way of life, a religious destiny. The problem with making peoplehood alone a self-sufficient value is that, with Jews across the world sharing neither a common language, nor land, nor culture, nor belief, peoplehood itself stands in need of explanation. In the absence of tradition, Jewish peoplehood dissolves into a variety of subcultures, brought together only at moments of crisis. (Sacks, 1995, p. 235)

Telling the story of the Holocaust itself is now of course to contribute to the answer to the question 'Who are the Jews?' As Sacks put it, 'Every Jew, after Auschwitz, knows that in some sense he is a survivor, an accidental remnant, and he shares that knowledge with every member of his people' (Sacks, 1995, p. 241).

Many of the rituals and festivals of the Jewish faith involve telling and retelling the story of the relationship between the Israelites (in other words the Jewish people) and God. The events of the Holocaust have become a part of this story and an important part of the Jewish sense of identity. Interestingly, the question of Jewish identity is included in the *Model Syllabuses for Religious Education* produced by the Qualifications and Curriculum Authority (QCA, 1998). These models were designed as a framework for those involved in drawing up RE syllabuses in local education authorities in England and Wales. They were first produced by the National Curriculum Council in 1994 and they are now having a significant influence on the approach and content of local authority syllabuses. In these model syllabuses the guidelines for teaching about Judaism suggest that students aged 11–14 should be encouraged to consider Jewish identity as expressed through the 'Jewish vision for the future; Israel today; Cultural diversity; Religious diversity past and present; Responses to racism; and the Jewish contribution to a just society' (QCA, 1998, p. 43). If these model syllabuses continue to inform the development of religious education in England and Wales, many students will be involved in looking at Judaism and the question of Jewish identity in their study of religion.

Why is it particularly important for pupils to look at the religious beliefs and practices of the Jews in preparation for Holocaust education? In some schools there is no teaching on world religions and so any work on the Holocaust may in fact be the first formal introduction to the Jewish people that students receive. If this is the case, it is likely that the Jews will appear from the beginning in the role of victim and there is a danger that this negative image will serve to reinforce stereotypes. Challenging stereotypes requires the teacher to ensure that the pupils receive positive images of the Jewish people to counter the negative messages they may receive from other sources. One opportunity for presenting the Jewish people in a positive light is through an introduction to the beliefs and practices of Judaism and in many schools in the UK this will take place in religious education. The first religion which students learn about after Christianity will usually be Judaism. For example, in primary schools students may begin by looking at life in the Jewish home and explore some of the festivals of the Jewish year. They will look at the scrolls of the Torah, learn stories from the Jewish scriptures and understand that Jews believe in One God. Later they may find out about Israel, the synagogue, bar mitzvah and the Jewish wedding ceremony. Through this religious education students can build up knowledge and understanding of Judaism and the richness of the faith and culture of the Jewish community will serve as a vivid backdrop against which the stark images from the Holocaust story will stand in meaningful contrast.

Another reason for ensuring that students have a background knowledge of the Jewish religion is that it enables them to understand the significance of many of the key events of the Holocaust. They need to know what a synagogue is and why it is important to the life of the Jewish community if they are going to understand the significance of Kristallnacht. They need to learn about the place and importance of the scriptures and sacred writings of the Jewish tradition if they are to realize the meaning of the burning of Jewish books as it is expressed in the following quotation from a Jewish child remembering:

> They are burning our books ... The Torah scrolls! The fire is dancing a bizarre dance of death with one large scroll in the middle, twisting and turning ... aged folios of Jewish wisdom and faith tumble and explode into fiery particles, spluttering pellets of ash. Volumes of the Bible, leatherbound Psalms, Tefillin, turn and twist and burst ... pictures and documents flutter as weightless speckles of ash at the edge of the savage torch. Our identity ... our soul ... weightless speckles of ash rising, fleeing the flames into nothingness. (Tatelbaum, 1985, p. 41)

Students who are encouraged to recognize the Jews as individuals, as well as the Jews as a people, are more likely to be moved by the events of the Holocaust. An essential part of an individual's identity is their beliefs and their religion. Students who know how Shabbat is celebrated in the home, how the young Jewish boy prepares for bar mitzvah and how the Jewish couple view marriage are more likely to see the Jews as people like themselves with beliefs, hopes and aspirations for the future – in other words as individuals. Students can explore the relationship between their own personal beliefs and their sense of who they are. They can then examine the religious beliefs and traditions of the Jewish community and the way in which these are an important part of their sense of identity.

Many teachers in religious education believe that learning about Judaism can have an important part to play in overcoming antisemitism. Antisemitism is still a problem in schools and in society at large. There is no simple explanation for antisemitism. Indeed, it is not easy to explain the workings of any form of prejudice; prejudice of this sort may serve different functions in different personalities and in different societies. However, it is possible that some antisemitism has its roots in ignorance and misunderstanding. Many teachers in religious education believe that developing the students' knowledge and understanding of Judaism may help to dislodge stereotypes and challenge some forms of prejudice. They hope that in presenting a positive image of the people and their religious tradition, they may help to prevent some of the misunderstanding and thereby play a part in reducing antisemitism. Some approaches to teaching about Judaism begin by exploring areas of shared concern and common values. For example, students in primary school looking at the Jewish home might explore the way in which the Jewish family keeps a kosher kitchen. They might then be encouraged to contribute to the class discussion something of the rules and traditions in their own home regarding food, cooking and eating. In this way, learning about the Jewish way of life raises opportunities for emphasizing shared human concerns as well as exploring those things that are distinctive to the Jewish community. In work in secondary schools, students are encouraged to look at Jewish perspectives on current issues. For example they may look at the importance of protecting the environment and learn that according to Jewish law, every seventh year the land must lie fallow and whatever grows there is ownerless. Young people have their own views on the state of the environment and other important issues. Through looking at Jewish perspectives on them students may find shared concerns. If students receive some background on the religious life and practice of the Jewish people they must of course find out what is unique and distinctive about the Jewish tradition and this is certainly the overall aim and the approach now taken in many RE syllabuses. However, most teachers would say that they also want their students to be able to identify shared concerns and values.

There are different dimensions to the Holocaust, for example, the historical and the political dimensions. There is also the literature of the Holocaust, the moral dimension and the issues of persecution and racism. These different dimensions make the subject suited to cross-curricular work in schools. However, the religious dimension is often left out or given insufficient attention. Without the religious dimension pupils will be unable to piece together the many parts of the puzzle. An important part of the religious background is the history of anti-Jewish feeling and religious persecution perpetrated by the Christian church. This background is usually given space in the telling of the story of antisemitism. On the whole, less time and attention has been given to the religious dimension in terms of the beliefs and traditions of the Jewish people and the part these have played in the way the Jews have survived the experience and interpreted the events of the Holocaust. It is impossible to reduce 3500 years of a religion and culture into a single chapter and any faith reduced to a series of bullet points will be a distortion. So there is no attempt here to try to give a potted version of the Jewish religion. There are now many well-written and attractive textbooks on Judaism produced by or with the help of members of the faith community that teachers may use for their own background knowledge and for work with their students. Instead of a summary of the faith, the rest of this chapter sets out four key issues regarding the teaching of Judaism: first, the legacy of old-style religious instruction in school, second, the importance of presenting Judaism as a living religion, third, Judaism and diversity including Judaism as a world religion, and fourth, Judaism and young people.

First, teachers are having to take seriously the legacy of the negative press that Judaism received through traditional approaches to religious instruction in British schools in years gone by. In the majority of schools in years past, and unfortunately in a handful of schools still today, teachers of religious instruction have approached the story of the Jews from a narrow, Christian perspective. The traditional assumption was that Judaism had been superseded by Christianity, the Jewish people had rejected the Messiah, Judaism had therefore lost its way and was a religion without hope and lacking in a sense of direction and purpose. The uncritical use of Gospel stories read in classrooms across the UK helped to reinforce the stereotype of the Jews as blind to the truth, narrowly focused on the requirements of petty laws and ultimately, responsible for the death of Jesus. It is essential that teachers are aware of this legacy and take seriously the problems arising from uncritical reading of the gospel texts if these stereotypes are to be avoided. The story of the crucifixion needs particular care and sensitivity and it is good to see that there are now versions of the Gospel stories, suitable for use in schools, which have been written in such a way as to avoid the negative stereotyping of the Jews. There is now a growing sensitivity among the publishers of school textbooks with regard to the question of the anti-Jewish language in the gospel narratives and there are versions now which use language that would not be offensive to Jewish children participating in their school RE lesson on the story of the crucifixion.

Another legacy of the traditional approach to religious instruction in schools is the way in which the Jewish teaching on the nature of God is portrayed. The often expressed view is that the Jewish God is a stern and unforgiving God, standing in judgement over the world and ready to punish those who break his commandments whereas the Christian God is perceived as a God of forgiveness. Reinforcing this idea is the Christian view of the Old and New Testaments – often taken to suggest a development from the belief that God was a God of doom and destruction to God as a God of love. This over-simplification and misrepresentation is very damaging in terms of building understanding between Christians and Jews; it is also unhelpful in terms of the need to present a positive introduction to the Jewish faith to students in schools. Such a common distortion of the Jewish view of God is based on a misunderstanding of the nature of the Torah. The written Torah, which Christians call the Old Testament, is not meant to be swallowed whole without its interpretation. The Jewish understanding of Torah includes both written and oral Torah. In the oral Torah (the Mishnah, Talmud, etc.) we find that the command-ments are interpreted with so much compassion and good sense that it might be said that God often errs on the side of being too forgiving. It is therefore important that in presenting the Jewish faith students have the opportunity to hear examples of the oral tradition alongside their study of the written Torah. In this way they will receive a more accurate picture of the Jewish perspective on the nature of God and his relationship with the world.

Another stereotypical view which continues to burden us from the legacy of the past is the image of the Jews having a narrow focus on the details of the Torah. If students are to receive a positive impression of Judaism, teachers need to present the faith as a religion of the heart and not just a religion based on keeping laws. The stereotype of the Jew being trapped in a routine of narrow-minded law keeping has its roots in the Gospel stories. Many school textbooks reinforced this view of Judaism as a religion made up of rules:

> In addition to the Ten Commandments there are over 600 laws – laws of marriage, crime and punishment, what to eat and what not to eat, religious practices, holy days and other matters ... the study of, and the living by the rules, as set out in the Torah is the most important part of the Jewish religion. (Meade and Zimmermann, 1966, p. 16)

Fortunately, textbooks are now beginning to present a much more positive introduction to Judaism. However, there is still a tendency to dwell on the number of the commandments and to present the Torah as if it were simply a book of rules. For example, in teaching about Judaism in Key Stage 1, in the early years of primary school one recent RE syllabus suggests that:

> Pupils should be encouraged to think about: the need for rules, rules which are important to them and the difference between right and wrong; the Torah: guidance and stories and rules which set out how people should live, the Ten Commandments, love your neighbour as yourself (Leviticus 19) and stories from the Tenach e.g. Joseph and his brothers. (QCA, 1998, p. 19)

Practice in schools, however, is changing for the better; for example, in the past, when students learnt about how the Jews keep Shabbat, the version they received gave the impression that Shabbat was a very negative experience and the emphasis was on what the Jews were not allowed to do. Shabbat is welcomed in the Jewish home and current students learning about this important festival will focus on the celebration meal on Friday evenings. They are more likely to watch on video the Jewish mother lighting the candles, have an opportunity to taste the challah bread and listen to the prayers that are sung rather than write a list of all the things that are not permitted on the Sabbath.

To turn to the second point, and this is closely related to the first, it is essential to present Judaism as a living religion. In the days when religious education was based on Bible study, Judaism was often equated with the Old Testament. The result was that Jews were presented as people of the past. For many students, their knowledge of Judaism was limited to what they learnt through the study of the Bible. In schools all over the UK, hours of the RE syllabus were spent on tracing maps of ancient Israel, drawing diagrams of the temple, listing kings and prophets and looking at 'life in Old Testament times'. No doubt there are some, including perhaps members of the Jewish community, who would be happy to have this approach to RE reinstated in schools. However, if students learn about the Jewish tradition only through the Old Testament approach, they are encouraged to see Judaism as a religious way of life trapped in the past. Students learning about Judaism need to see how the Jewish community expresses its faith now, in the home, in the synagogue, in the wider world and in everyday life as well as on the special occasions. It is therefore important that teachers select their resources carefully. It is now easy to find textbooks that introduce Judaism through the life of the contemporary community. However, some books still take a historical approach and begin with the stories of Abraham and Moses from the Tenakh, the Jewish Bible. Some syllabuses take a balanced approach so that pupils are introduced to the stories from the scriptures – for example the seven days of creation – while also looking at how the Jewish family now celebrates Shabbat and remembers the seventh day of creation as a day of rest. The photographs, pictures and audiovisual material we use with students have an important part to play in terms of the image of Judaism we want to present. In the past some publishers had difficulties in getting up-to-date photographs of Jewish religious practices because of the personal nature of some of the images; contemporary photographs of family occasions and religious rituals in the home were particularly hard to come by. Times are changing and there are now excellent visual resources available which reflect the contemporary face of Judaism and teachers should be well equipped to present a positive image of the faith. Judaism has much to offer older students in terms of exploring different perspectives on current issues. Using articles from Jewish newspapers and journals can help to emphasize the place and importance of Judaism in the world today. Taking account of the contribution of the Jewish voice in political and moral discourse on racism, immigration, human rights, medical ethics, environmental concerns and other issues facing humanity is essential if we are to reflect the different voices in our multi-faith and multicultural society.

Third, it is important to present the diversity within Judaism. In this way students will see the complexity of the question 'Who are the Jews?' The textbook version of a religion often comes pre-packaged with the difficulties and differences smoothed out; sometimes this means that we are not presenting a realistic picture of the tradition. In fact it is helpful for students to see the diversity within a religious community. Hearing the different voices from within the faith, the student is given the opportunity to get more than one perspective and this opens up opportunities for greater understanding and interest. Some of the divisions within Judaism run very deep. Orthodox Judaism, for example, has maintained the belief in the divine origin of the Torah. The Reform movement and many within the Conservative movement recognize the Torah as the work of human hearts and minds and interpret the commandments in the light of what is known about the world today. Orthodoxy regards members of Reform Judaism as non-believers because they reject the divine origin of the Torah. If students are not made aware of the diversity within the tradition there is a danger that the one Jewish person they meet in life will become the model from which they will judge Judaism in its entirety. Once familiar with the diversity within the tradition, the student will be in a better position to interpret the voices of the Jews they meet and put their particular perspectives into context. The diversity within Judaism is not simply a matter of difference in theology; there are also differences in terms of practice. Some of these differences have arisen as a result of the Jewish people being dispersed across the world. It is essential that students see the richness and diversity within the tradition and the way in which the religious practice has developed in different ways in different parts of the globe. An understanding of the Sephardic, the Ashkenazic and the Yemenite communities will help students to see Judaism as a world religion which crosses the boundaries of country and culture. This approach may also help to break down some of the myths and stereotypes associated with the idea of a Jewish race. In the QCA model syllabuses for example, students in religious education in secondary schools are expected to look at:

> Ways in which members of groups and communities can be similar and different and in developing their knowledge and understanding of Judaism they are encouraged to look at Israel and related issues including Immigrant absorption; Cultural and religious diversity; Maintaining Jewish identity; The Anglo Jewish experience. (QCA, 1998, p. 43)

Fourth, it is important to represent Judaism as a religion for young people. Many of the images of the faith reflect a tradition of an older generation – the scribe with the long white beard, copying out the scrolls of the Torah, is one of the classic images of Judaism. And of course in telling the story of the Holocaust, the survivors will all be from an older generation. It is essential that students hear the young voices within the faith. There are now good videos available for schools where young people talk about their beliefs and practices. In many primary schools the study of Judaism is introduced through the festivals. This approach has the advantage of providing opportunities for exploring the faith through the eyes of the children. Many of the traditions and customs associated with the festivals are designed to involve children and young people in telling and re-enacting important events from the religious history of the Israelites (the Jewish People). For example, at the Seder meal at Pesach (Passover) it is traditional for the youngest child present to play a key role in the service by asking the question 'Why is this night different from all other nights?' This is the opening line for the telling of the story of the journey from slavery to freedom. At the celebration of the festival of Sukkot Jewish children look forward to the opportunity to sleep out under the stars in the Sukkah (shelter) they have built to remember the time that the Children of Israel were in the wilderness. During the synagogue service held at the popular festival of Purim the children shake rattles, biscuit-tins full of nails and anything else that will make a noise to drown out the name of the villain Haman in the telling of the story of Queen Esther. As the prayer book says: 'In the days of Mordechai and Esther, in Shushan the capital, when the wicked Haman rose up against them, he sought to destroy, kill and exterminate all the Jews, both young and old, little children and women, on one day, and plunder their possessions.' This approach – an introduction to Judaism through the festivals and holy days of the tradition – is an important and helpful way in which to prepare students for looking at the events of the Holocaust. It encourages an awareness of a way of life that they can recognize as having value and meaning for children and young people – a way of life that could have been lost for ever. In many schools the *Diary of Anne Frank* is adopted as an approach to the study of the Holocaust because it is written from the point of view of a young person with hopes and dreams not unlike those of many young people today. The story of Anne Frank will be given greater significance and depth if the students are familiar with aspects of the Jewish home and the way of life that would have been part of her everyday experience. Religious education can make a very valuable contribution to teaching and learning about the Holocaust in laying these foundations of knowledge and understanding of the Jewish traditions and way of life.

The study of Judaism has a part to play in promoting opportunities for greater intercultural awareness, dialogue and co-operation in a multi-faith and multicultural society. Certainly, many religious education teachers were in broad agreement with the brave claims of the Swann Report (1985) that: 'Religious education can play a central role in preparing all pupils for life in today's multi-racial Britain, and can also lead them to a greater understanding of the diversity of the global community' (Swann Report, 1985, p. 496).

In some schools, the department of religious education establishes strong links with the local faith communities through developing a programme of visits and visitors. Many religious education programmes now include a visit to the synagogue in their scheme of work on Judaism. This provides the opportunity for the students to see Judaism as a living faith. The students may have a chance to meet with members of the faith community and to see them on their home ground. In this situation the students are encouraged to feel that doors are open, that barriers are down and that they are able to ask questions and enter into dialogue with a member of the community. The religious education teacher may also invite a member of the faith into the school to talk about Judaism in the home or to lead a presentation of Pesach Seder, the Passover meal. In this way links are forged with the local Jewish community and students begin to develop a rich resource of positive experiences in RE, providing sound foundations for building on later. With this background knowledge and understanding and these valuable encounters with the Jewish community – established through a coherent programme of religious education – when the students do come to study the Holocaust and the teacher asks 'Who are the Jews?', the students will be able to give a meaningful answer.

REFERENCES

Meade, F.H.M. and Zimmermann, A.W. (1966) *Religions of the World*, School Study Bible Series. Edinburgh: Holmes McDougall.

Qualifications and Curriculum Authority (QCA) (1998) *Model Syllabuses for Religious Education* (Model 2). London: QCA.

Sacks, J. (1995) *Faith in the Future*. London: Darton, Longman and Todd.

Swann Report (1985) *Education for All: The Report of the Committee of Inquiry into the Education of Children from Ethnic Minority Groups*. London: HMSO.

Tatelbaum, I. (1985) *Through Our Eyes: Children Witness the Holocaust*. Jerusalem: IBT Publishing.

Chapter 3

The Holocaust: Some Reflections and Issues

Ian Gregory

The Holocaust is a moral outrage almost beyond the comprehension of the individual mind. The bare rehearsal of the number of Jews slaughtered on no other grounds than that they were Jews beggars the imagination. Even allowing for the technical difficulties confronting the efforts to precisely enumerate the individuals killed as a consequence of their Jewish origins (Hilberg, 1989, p. 155), we can say with confidence that about 6 million individuals perished as the Nazis sought a 'final solution' to the Jewish 'problem'. We also know with an equal measure of confidence that in addition to the Jews, another 5 million or so non-Jews were killed by the technology of mass destruction put in place by the Nazis as they pursued the extermination of Jewry in its entirety. We are in the presence of a moral outrage encompassing so many victims that it is impossible to fully grasp – even start to grasp, one feels tempted to say – the significance of what we are being told. To know that so many individuals were pitilessly put to death is one thing, to feel and appreciate the significance of such a tragedy is another. But we must try. If we come to grasp how and why human beings can treat others on such a massive scale with such callousness and brutality we might perhaps be better placed, if not to avoid, at least to limit recurrences of similar outrages.

We need to remember that two-thirds of European Jewry did not survive the Nazi onslaught, that wherever the German rule in Europe was total, the annihilation of Jews was correspondingly total. East European Jewry was all but obliterated and with it a vital and distinctive Jewish culture. We should fully appreciate that as from early 1942 – whatever the exact intentions of the Nazis in the matter of the genocide of the Jews before that time – the decision was made that the Jews had no right to live. To that end the Nazi state was dedicated to the destruction of an entire people. If the Nazis had been victorious in the Second World War, the Jews would have disappeared off the face of the earth.

It is not for nothing that the Holocaust – used henceforth to designate the systematic and determined slaughter of the Jews and others with a view to their final extirpation from the races of the world – has been seen as the defining moment of modern history, perhaps of all time. It is not for nothing that fearful of what has been seen and experienced, such effort has been given to trying to understand its significance, learn its lessons (if any). Our concerns arise from the fact that genocide and related evils cannot be perpetrated unless there are significant numbers of individuals lending their support to governments bent on genocide, the massacre of thousands, the harassment of minority groups, unless there are those who are willing to do what is required to kill or harass those whose fate it is to be killed or harassed because they are members of some disfavoured group. What is generally true was as true of the Nazi genocide. And it is specifically to the issues raised by this most awful moment in history we now turn. The importance of such reflection can scarcely be doubted.

> That which has happened is a warning. To forget it is guilt. It must be continually remembered. It was possible for this to happen, and it remains possible for it to happen again at any minute. Only in knowledge can it be prevented. (Jaspers, 1953, p. 149)

KEY ISSUES ARISING FROM REFLECTIONS ON THE HOLOCAUST

In the immediate aftermath of the war almost nothing was written on this direst of tragedies. It was as if, stunned by the recognition of the violence done to the canons of civilized behaviour, no one dared talk of what had happened. The literature on the Holocaust is, therefore, of relatively recent origins but is huge and shows no signs of abating. For our purposes it will be divided into two broad categories: that which seeks an explanation of how such an event could have transpired, and that which looks to the significance of the Holocaust for us as human beings, individually and socially as we struggle precariously to live with each other.

This most peculiar of Jewish tragedies, the vilest of the many expressions of rampant antisemitism of the past two thousand years, has not surprisingly attracted the attention of Jewish scholars – historians, philosophers, theologians, artists and critics, educationalists, political scientists, depth psychologists – like no other. It is within this internal debate of coming to terms with the Holocaust and its significance that so many of the most important debates around the Holocaust have surfaced. Two issues of fundamental importance are those of the uniqueness and the incomprehensibility of the Holocaust. It is important to appreciate that claims about both the uniqueness and the incomprehensibility of the Nazi genocide are separate claims and must be kept apart. Even if, in some specified sense, an event is unique, it might nevertheless be rendered comprehensible (suitably understood). Even if an event is incomprehensible, it might not transpire to be unique.

The claim to uniqueness is the claim that in substantial and relevant ways the Holocaust is like no other event there has previously been in history. The emphasis upon what has previously been the case clearly allows for the possibility that it could happen again. Indeed it is precisely this awareness that what has happened (uniquely) once might happen again that has encouraged the determination of Jews and all right-minded people that it must never happen again. The cry 'never again' expresses the aspiration that not only the Jews but also any other group (racial, ethnic or cultural) should never be exposed to policies that, for whatever reason, determine to destroy an entire group of people for no reason other than that they are. In part, teaching about the Holocaust seeks to make it less likely that such tragedies should recur.

The term 'incomprehensibility' suggests that which is in the last resort inexplicable, not capable of being understood. In terms of the events of the Holocaust the claim is that despite all of our efforts, we must retreat baffled by the enormity of the Holocaust. As Fackenheim (1978, p. 93) characteristically puts it: 'despite all the necessary attempts to comprehend it, the Nazi system in the end exceeds all comprehension. One cannot comprehend but only confront and object'. The implications of such an approach cast a deep shadow over the hope that we might give substance to the cry 'never again'. If it is literally humanly incomprehensible we are denied the possibility of trying to avert such a calamity again. We need to look more closely at this claim of incomprehensibility. The very possibility of teaching about the Holocaust as part of an educational programme depends on resisting a literal reading of the Holocaust as incomprehensible.

The second dimension of our concern with the Holocaust is what it tells us about humans as moral and political creatures – how we conduct our lives at the individual and social level with reference to others and their independent interests.

At the most general level the challenge posed by the Holocaust, and in the starkest manner by the extermination camps of Auschwitz, Sobibor, Treblinka, Chelmno, Belzec and Majdanek, is whether the belief in the possibilities of moral progress on the part of humankind can be shown finally to be a chimera, a figment of unrealistic minds – minds refusing to face up to the intrinsic nature of human beings. It is a characteristic of many political philosophies that over time a transformation in moral consciousness is at least possible. A combination of juster political systems, better education, higher standards of living, a more profound understanding of the main-springs of human action will, it has been thought, encourage a greater awareness of the claims of others upon us, diminish the amount of violence in human affairs. In short, progress is as possible in the quality of our moral dealings as it so palpably is in the other areas of human knowledge and understanding. Such a perspective finds its clearest articulation in doctrines such as the natural goodness of man and the perfectibility of human beings. But the belief in moral progress does not need to be yoked to any such very strong doctrinal commitments. It is enough to believe that a measure of moral progress is feasible. The Holocaust in all of its abominations has been viewed as challenging even such a more modest optimism.

At the individual level, the Holocaust forces us to confront the complex of issues surrounding responsibility. We know that without the support and acquiescence of large numbers of 'ordinary' Germans and other Europeans, the wholesale slaughter of Jews and others in the concentration and death camps could not have proceeded so easily to its tragic outcome. The issues of moral indifference, failing to stand up and be counted, being a bystander to such appalling events, need to be addressed with a view to understanding better the nature of the responsibility humans enjoy one for the other.

Issues of morality and politics often touch each other in all kinds of ways. One of the hardest issues to understand – and which should always be a salutary reminder to ourselves never to be too sanguine about the present – is how was it possible that Germany, which had produced a culture that was one of the great glories of European civilization, should so easily lend itself to the ends of such a murderous and barbarous regime. To understand (to whatever degree it is possible to understand) such a phenomenon seems imperative if any lessons are to be learnt that might aid us in the future. Even if the gloomiest readings of the significance of the Holocaust are rejected, it must always stand as a reminder of how important it is that we cling hard to all those moral sentiments, values, principles and outlooks that the Nazis turned their back on and with such dire consequences. The next section of this chapter will say a little more about the issues thus far raised.

FURTHER REFLECTIONS ON THE UNIQUENESS, INCOMPREHENSIBILITY AND MORAL SIGNIFICANCE OF THE HOLOCAUST

Estimates of the numbers killed in the Second World War vary. It seems likely that at least 30–35 million died and maybe that the number killed was as high as 50 million. They died in all kinds of ways and in all parts of the world where the war was waged. The Soviet Union suffered the greatest losses – perhaps as many as 20 million – mainly in combat but we know with a fair degree of accuracy that about 3.5 million Soviet prisoners of war were killed by the Germans either in the death camp of Auschwitz, or in various ways gunned down. Poland's losses were of the order of 6–7 million, about 22 per cent of the pre-war population. Of those Poles killed, about 3 million were Jews. Yugoslavia lost about 9 per cent of its population (some 1.5 million individuals). Losses in western Europe were significantly less, with France suffering the greatest percentage loss at 1.5 per cent of its pre-war population. It is within such a context of massive slaughter that the issues of the uniqueness, incomphrehensibility and moral significance of the Holocaust have to be set.

What was it about the Nazi genocide of the Jews that sets it (still?) apart from any other genocidal slaughter in history? In what ways is the Holocaust incomprehensible? What are the values, sentiments, principles and outlooks the rejection of which the Holocaust symbolizes? What are the lessons we should heed to try and avert such dark times again? And can schooling and education play a part in the effort to ensure 'never again'?

The last question highlights that the most radical threat to the learning of lessons that might be heeded as we struggle to make a better world, locally, nationally and internationally, is the issue of the alleged incomprehensibility of the Holocaust. If in all crucial respects, or even in some crucial respects, it cannot be comprehended, we are denied important possibilities of understanding that might be utilized in the fight for a better world. Even if the Holocaust is unique, this is not to say it cannot be comprehended or that important elements shared in common with other humanly inspired great evils cannot be recognized as part of the unique event that is the Nazi genocide.

We surely know, and recent historians affirm it, that 'the distinguishing characteristic of Nazi Germany was its obsession with race' (Burleigh, 1997, p. 155). It was not, as has been remarked, that the Nazis were racists because they were anti-Semitic. It was rather that antisemitism was a particularly virulent expression of an all-pervasive racism that also affected other groups within society apart from the Jews. Without going as far as the Goldhagen (1996) thesis that pretty well indicts most 'ordinary Germans' as embracing the peculiarly virulent variant of antisemitism that distinguished Hitler's outlook – what Goldhagen calls 'eliminationist antisemitism' – there is plenty of evidence to suggest that important sectors of German society of the time (doctors, psychiatrists, historians, economists and the like) who were crucial to the pursuit and operationalizing of the Nazi persecution of the Jews and other groups who suffered so grievously at the hands of the German state shared in the racism of the time.

The claim as to the uniqueness of the Holocaust is not in any way to diminish the terrible sufferings of non-Jews who found themselves victims of the racist theories of the Nazis. It is to claim that within the category of those who found themselves suspect because of the racist fantasies of the time that enjoyed such wide currency within certain circles in Germany, the Jews were particularly singled out and stigmatized in ways different from other groups. The policy pursued in respect of the Jews was of a different order from that of any other group – even the Gypsies who as a group were also singled out for special attention.

The exact connection between the decision to wage the Second World War and the war against Jewry as an expression of the desire to rid the world of the Jew so as to make the world a fit place for humans to live in, is much discussed. But what is clear is that whenever it was decided, the complete and systematic elimination of Jews became the cardinal feature of Nazi policy. So much so that even when it was clear the war was lost, ever greater exhortation and effort to destroy Jews was evident. 'What was unique in the Holocaust was the totality of its ideology and of its translation of abstract thought into planned, logically implemented total murder' (Bauer, 1989, p. 18). 'The murder of the Jews and the destruction of Jewish communal existence were ... in contrast ends in themselves, ultimate goals to which the National Socialist state had dedicated itself' (Dawidowicz, 1989, p. 60). The racism that was so chronic a feature of the Nazi mentality showed itself in the policies adopted towards the Czechs, Poles, Ukrainians, Russians, Lithuanians, Latvians and Estonians. As inferior groups they were to be bent to the German will through Germanization, deportation, slavery, intimidation through violence and murder, the destruction of their political leadership, and so on. But it was never envisaged that they should be annihilated simply by virtue of being. They were viewed as inferior human beings rather than being written out of the human story entirely.

Even the tragic story of the Gypsies at the hands of the Nazis, the nearest equivalent to the treatment of the Jews, has elements about it that allow for a distinction to be drawn not between the moral evil inflicted upon them but rather the motivation informing policy towards them. We know too little of their story. We do know of the great slaughter of the Gypsies in Yugoslavia and Poland and exactly how many were killed in Auschwitz (2897). Estimates of the overall death count of the Gypsy vary between 500,000 to upwards of 1 million. But we know that despite the application to the Gypsy of the same ideology informing policy and practice and their fate at the hands of the same SS (*Schutzstaffel* – Nazi elite corps), they were not entirely written out of the human race. 'Pure' Gypsies could live. Racially impure Gypsies alone had to die. And their destruction was more fitfully pursued and not a defining feature of National Socialism as a world-view.

Whether the foregoing is enough to sustain the idea of the uniqueness of the Holocaust as an event in history is one thing. What it does not do is establish the Holocaust as a uniquely evil act. It is difficult to justify the suggestion that the evil inflicted upon the Jews is of a different order from that inflicted on all those other groups who so suffered under the Nazi regime. In addition to the groups already mentioned, we must add those who had all their rights tramped upon, mentally ill people, homosexuals, prostitutes, physically infirm and physically handicapped people, petty criminals, the victims of medical experimentation and all those who were the victims of 'euthanasia' as an arm of government policy. In the dangerous fantasy world of the 'Pure Aryan' as the highest expression of the possibilities of humanity, it should occasion little surprise that those who in obvious enough ways offended the moral and physical sensibilities of the favoured ones would find themselves the victims of legislation and policies bent on purifying the genetic stock of the chosen race.

It is understanding the nature of the evil commonly shared by all the victims of the Nazi state that affords us the opportunity to conceptualize our sense of what we should strive to do to avert such possibilities in the future. The 'final solution' to the 'Jewish problem' might indeed be a unique event in history but yet be of universal significance in that it tells us what we all need to cling on to if morality is going to play the guiding role we look to it to play in the 'amelioration of the human predicament'. But we first need to establish that comprehensibility of the Holocaust is a possibility itself.

Talk of the incomprehensibility of the Holocaust is not all of a piece. Different propositions claim our allegiance. If the claim is that there will never be a historical explanation which finally resolves any problem that might arise in connection with the Holocaust, this does not seem in principle to place the Holocaust on a different footing from any other great historical event. The French Revolution still attracts as much historical attention as was ever the case, and no one seems particularly exercised that no single account commends itself to all historians. This is not thought to entail that we should give up on the endeavour to understand the French Revolution. Nor indeed, is it thought that our understanding of the French Revolution is radically defective or of no worth because room for disagreement remains. We simply strive for a more adequate understanding where we feel there is more to be understood: we seek to understand as well as we are able.

If the claim is that in principle no light can be cast on the events of the Holocaust, there is no reason to believe the claim to be true. Even while we struggle with the enormity of the crime that is the Holocaust, as history, there is no reason to doubt the significance of debates between historians about the cause of this or that element that makes up the story of the Holocaust. There seems no reason to doubt that as a consequence of the efforts of historians, we have more or less adequate understandings of how it was Hitler rose to power, carrying the German nation with him and what he hoped to achieve in pursuing this or that policy. If we want to understand his antisemitism, intellectual historians are able to indicate those sources that shaped his key ideas. We may wish to understand more profoundly the determining instances of an event of such magnitude, but there seems no insuperable barrier to such historical understanding. Such understanding might highlight, so we might think, what should be borne in mind in the future so as to avoid or diminish the recurrence of such an outrage.

In terms of lessons to be learnt, the more disturbing claim might be that the incomprehensibility of the Holocaust resides in the inadequacy of our moral concepts to make sense of what has happened. So far removed from our normal moral experience and expectations is the Holocaust and its events that a moral framework fit for our more everyday experiences cannot adequately characterize the moral quality of the Holocaust. It sometimes seems to be suggested that to render the Holocaust comprehensible, we need to forge another vocabulary fit for the purpose. Why this is such a disturbing proposition is that until we forge a new and appropriate vocabulary, whatever it might be to do such a thing, we are consigned to silence and unable to talk constructively about the Holocaust. Unable to talk about the Nazi genocide of the Jews, we lack the wherewithal to devise programmes of learning designed to promote young people wedded to positive values acting as a barrier to outlooks and ways of treating others reminiscent of the Holocaust. To teach constructively and usefully about the Holocaust demands an ability on our part, while recognizing the peculiarly Jewish dimension of the tragedy, to discern its more universal elements. Luckily there is no reason to accept that our ordinary moral discourse – in all of its diversity and richness – cannot characterize the moral outrage that is the Holocaust.

The most perplexing thing about the Holocaust is not how to conceptualize what went on but that what was done, was done. How to explain that educated people, ordinary (in the usual run of things) Germans lent themselves so enthusiastically to butchering fellow human beings? How to explain the passive acquiescence in the face of implicit knowledge of what was being done in the name of Germany? Goldhagen (1996) reminds us that as revealing as the fact that so many were destroyed is how they were destroyed. How can one come to terms with men eagerly swinging young children around in front of their parents and dashing their skulls against walls, with drowning humans in pits of human excrement and urine, with telling a father to shoot his sons, bury their bodies and then instructing him to carry on digging despite one of the children still being alive, or throwing live children into the crematoria? One could endlessly multiply stories of unimaginable cruelty and depravity. Unless it had happened, one could not imagine such things could go on. Knowing they happened, however, poses the task of coming to understand how they could.

Morally we can accurately represent the Holocaust. The descriptions that capture the fate of the Jews are as readily applicable to the other minorities who so suffered at the hands of the Nazis. In giving moral characterizations, we spell out the key moral values any programme teaching about the Holocaust must stand as testament to. The Holocaust breaches the barriers put up by morality but our moral discourse can still describe and evaluate the nature of the barbarities practised. In understanding the values that were trampled on by the Nazi genocide we can reaffirm our determination to promote and encourage them through educational programmes.

What the Holocaust represents in the starkest terms imaginable is the final rupture of '... moral prohibitions, apparent barriers to action, which a man acknowledges and which he thinks of as more or less insurmountable, except in abnormal, painful and improbable circumstances' (Hampshire, 1978, p. 7). To challenge them is to challenge the very claims of morality itself. These prohibitions 'are forbidden as being intrinsically disgraceful and unworthy, and as being just for these reasons, ruled out: ruled out because they would be disgusting, or disgraceful, or shameful, or brutal, or inhuman, or base, or an outrage' (Hampshire, 1978, p. 77). To do these things makes anything possible. A relapse into barbarism beckons. What the Holocaust represents in the starkest terms imaginable is that final disrespect for other humans beyond which bestiality beckons. The key to understanding the moral outrage that the Holocaust embodies is that it gives up on any suggestion that fellow human beings not of the preferred group are worthy of equality of dignity and respect. In keeping with the fantasies of racism, all except the favoured ones are not to be viewed, using the language of Kant, as ends in themselves. They are simply means to the ends laid down by the superior group – to be disposed of as they see fit, and in the case of the Jews, written out of the human race altogether. With the rejection of the notion of equality of concern and respect also goes a whole discourse which fleshes out the implications of commitment to the inherent dignity of humans. To understand how a people can give up on a moral tradition which owes so much to Kant, the greatest of the moral philosophers and a German, might be a task beyond us. To understand how to pre-empt the radical evil that can accompany this disdain for other humans might be a task beyond us. We already live with the terrible fear that these final prohibitions which the Holocaust and the slaughter of the other 5 million non-Jews displayed such contempt for, far from acting as a warning against any repetition, have put genocide and the mass killing of others on the agenda as an increasingly common and integral feature of contemporary political life. To that extent we have learnt the lessons of history only too well.

Before we embrace such counsels of despair, however, we should look to see whether teaching about the Holocaust might offer us a way forward. As might be expected, the teaching of such a traumatic event in history poses peculiar problems. Some of these further issues are discussed in Chapter 4.

REFERENCES

Bauer, Y. (1989) The place of the Holocaust in contemporary history. In J.K. Roth and M. Berenbaum (eds) *Holocaust*. New York: Paragon House.

Burleigh, M. (1997) *Ethics and Extermination*. Cambridge: Cambridge University Press.

Dawidowicz, L. (1989) Thinking about the six million: facts, figures, perspectives. In K. Roth and M. Berenbaum (eds) *Holocaust*. New York: Paragon House.

Fackenheim, E. (1978) *The Jewish Return into History: Reflections in the Age of Auschwitz and a New Jerusalem*. New York: Schocken Books.

Goldhagen, D. (1996) *Hitler's Willing Executioners: Ordinary Germans and the Holocaust*. London: Little, Brown.

Hampshire, S. (ed.) (1978) *Public and Private Morality*. Cambridge: Cambridge University Press.

Hilberg, R. (1989) The statistic. In F. Furet (ed.) *Unanswered Questions*. New York: Schocken Books.

Jaspers, K. (1953) *The Origin and Goal of History*. New Haven, CT: Yale University Press.

Chapter 4

Teaching about the Holocaust: Perplexities, Issues and Suggestions

Ian Gregory

Perhaps we should not be surprised if teaching about the Holocaust poses peculiar and challenging questions. If not unique, if not incomprehensible, it is certainly a most singular event. The justification of why it should be studied in our schools is tribute to its singularity. We are all familiar with talk of activities being 'valuable in themselves', being 'worth doing for their own sake'. There is much to be said on the nature of such discourse and whether it can bear the weight placed upon it in the characterization of education, its aims and purposes. But it is often invoked in discussions justifying why the humanities, the pure sciences and mathematics are worthy of study and justifiably demanded as part of anyone's programme of education. The contrast is drawn with more consequentialist approaches. Consequentialist accounts justify the study of curricular subjects and topics because of certain kinds of outcomes – the needs of the economy, the development of certain character traits and so on.

Mention is made of these competing traditions because teaching about the Holocaust, one feels tempted to say, can be justified only by reference to its outcomes. There is something obscene, bearing in mind the enormity of the event, in the idea that it should be studied because it is valuable in itself. However, to ransack the Holocaust simply in order to highlight some point about historical method or explanation, even to highlight a point about prejudice and its role in human affairs, is to be too disrespectful of the victims of the Nazi genocide. To use the Holocaust to illustrate a point that could be made in so many other ways is deep down not to take it seriously enough for the outrage that it was. The act of teaching about the Holocaust should be commemorative of the suffering of all of those (Jews and non-Jews) butchered by the Nazi system of extermination. It reflects our determination that never again should such an atrocity be perpetrated. It is our way of investing their deaths with a certain meaning. To remain in awe of the event, to refuse to engage with it, is both wilfully to turn our backs on their suffering and degradation and by yet another kind of indifference to do nothing to avert the possibility of a repetition. If we teach about the Holocaust (certainly in schools) we should do so with the unwavering intent to do justice to its horrors and the lessons (if any) to be drawn from it.

To teach the Holocaust simply as history – another historical event like the French Revolution – is inadequate. What is to be learnt from the Holocaust about being human is what justifies studying the Holocaust, conscious all the time that it is unimaginable suffering and differing degrees of human wickedness and indifference that are the subject of study. Scholars of all kinds (historians, sociologists, political scientists, philosophers, theologians and literary critics) seek to cast light upon the Holocaust in its different facets. Effective teaching on this most sensitive and controversial topic draws upon the range of perspectives that different disciplines afford us and encourages young people to reflect deeply and unflinchingly on the implications of what is presented. Whatever else it is, the Holocaust is a public event that demands to be understood to the best of our ability just because it tells us so much about human potentialities. We must rescue what we can from it with a view to protecting all those principles, values, and sentiments we so loudly proclaim in the name of democracy and morality.

The study of the Holocaust is shot through with controversy. But as a controversial topic it stands rather apart from so many of those topics that get, uneasily, lumped together under the umbrella of 'controversial issues' in our schools. It is not just its sheer complexity. Conscious of the range of strongly held opinions in respect of issues such as abortion, euthanasia and homosexuality, and the intractable nature of the disagreements around them, we strive not to violate the right of each young person to make up their own mind. On all of these issues we accept that it is still possible for individuals of good will exercising their rational faculties to the fullest extent to end up disagreeing about what is right and wrong. By exposing young people to debate on such issues we hope to encourage the capacity for better reasoning and to engender a greater measure of tolerance towards those with whom they disagree. Within liberal circles the belief in tolerance is an unquestioned article of faith.

Tolerance and teaching about the Holocaust have an uneasy relationship. This ambivalence reflects an intrinsic feature of tolerance as a concept. Tolerance occupies a position somewhere between that which is intolerable (not to be tolerated) and that to which we are indifferent (have no feelings about). I say 'somewhere between' since the boundaries of the intolerable and the indifferent change over time and circumstances. Tolerance plays the role in our lives that it does because there are some things (opinions, values, sentiments, ways of life) about which we feel disapproval (largely moral) but which we go along with. Rather crudely, we live and let live. If I am entirely indifferent to homosexuality as a manifestation of human sexuality, it seems inappropriate to say I am tolerant of homosexuality. If I am, however, morally disapproving of homosexual relationships then I can exercise tolerance towards such relationships. Tolerance enjoys its natural home within a context of moral disapproval of others and how they conduct their life. But the emphasis upon tolerance itself might encourage a certain reluctance to pass judgement on even the intolerable and further the moral indifference that certainly was manifested throughout the Nazi reign of terror, and which even now is (perhaps) too evident.

In his penetrating study of the Nazi genocide Lang (1990) cites an instance in which while teaching a course on the concept of evil he introduced a number of his undergraduate students to Hannah Arendt's (1979) *Eichmann in Jerusalem* and Simon Wiesenthal's (1976) *The Sunflower*. The responses of his students startled and appalled him. Rather than addressing the evil of the Nazi genocide, his students raised a host of incidental questions about the trial of Eichmann himself. Were the Israelis right to arrest him overseas and bring him back to Israel for trial? Were they justified in executing him? In respect of Wiesenthal seeking answers to his question about whether he was justified in refusing to grant a dying SS soldier forgiveness for atrocities he had committed against Jews in a concentration camp, Lang's students suggested that there was no reason to suppose that the soldier was even a candidate for forgiveness as he was a product of his education and background, he was just a soldier carrying out his orders. There being no suggestion of responsibility, hence there was no suggestion of guilt. Lang draws the entirely persuasive conclusion that his students demonstrated too great a deference to the ideal of tolerance rather than recognizing the evil with which they were confronted. He draws the larger conclusion that there is a danger associated with the celebration of tolerance which is that it encourages the habit of not choosing, of not discriminating in the ways that particular judgements about the moral quality of action demand. The refusal to take a stand on substantive moral issues on the grounds of respecting the actions of other individuals as freely choosing, self-determining agents, too easily encourages moral indifference. Moral indifference offers no barrier to patterns of behaviour that offend against the dictates constituting the very core of morality, as the Holocaust only too bleakly reminds us. None of this is to suggest that the Holocaust should not stand as testament to the importance of tolerance as a prized human value or that the acceptance of other groups – religious, racial, ethnic or cultural – should not be affirmed through our study of the Holocaust. It is, however, to demand that in teaching about the Holocaust, its wickedness, brutalities and barbarisms, we proclaim that there are some ways of behaving, some ways of viewing others, that are morally intolerable and which should be resisted in whatever ways they manifest themselves. To do this does not commit us to implausibilities such as racism leads inevitably to genocide. It clearly does not. It is to say that racism in any of its different forms is not to be tolerated.

THE HOLOCAUST AS AN OBJECT OF STUDY

Of any subject area that might be included on the curriculum, certain questions inevitably present themselves. What is the rationale for curricular inclusion? What topics should be taught? To whom should they be taught? How should the topics be best delivered by teachers? All of these questions can justifiably be raised in connection with the teaching of the Holocaust in schools. What follows is a sketchy response to the first two questions.

As a preliminary, it has to be said that consonant with the very subject matter of the Holocaust teachers must approach the task of teaching the Holocaust seriously in deference to its subject matter and, perhaps to make the same point another way, determined to be well informed. The momentousness of the event demands nothing less. In short, this is not a teaching task to be undertaken lightly.

TOWARDS A RATIONALE

The Holocaust is surely the most important single event of the twentieth century. Even within the more general horrors of the Second World War with its 35–50 million dead, the systematic, bureaucratic nature of the slaughter directed to the 6 million Jews and (even if not to be conceptualized as part of the Holocaust) another 5 million non-Jews has a gratuitousness that sets it apart from whatever else was going on at the same time. Hope enjoins that we make it an object of shared understanding. It is not enough to inform about the Holocaust; our task is to educate young people about it. We should encourage an understanding of how it came about and what its significance was and, importantly, might be to us at the present time.

> We always live in the hope that through the study of the past we might illumine the present and the future. The study of such dark events is premised on the aspiration that [we] can gain a brutally harsh knowledge of [our] capabilities and tendencies, a self-knowledge that is a necessary condition for the prevention of the actualisation of [our] worst possibilities. (Magurshak, 1989, p. 430)

Pre-eminent among the disciplines aiding our understanding of the Holocaust is history. It is historical understanding which tells us what happened, describes the circumstances of its happening and grants us insight into why events transpired as they did. We look to history to provide us with the materials from which to derive lessons to be brought into public consciousness. The very precondition of learning from the Holocaust is an accurate appreciation of events, how and why they came about. Any rationale for teaching about the Holocaust needs to grant a proper recognition to the primacy of history as the source of information about the Holocaust upon which we can construct our unflattering image of what it is to be human.

THEMES FOR TEACHING ABOUT THE HOLOCAUST

Its history

The exercise of sound judgement is dependent on many things: a proper understanding of the nature of the judgements to be made, the exercise of the relevant intellectual skills upon the subject matter of the judgement, and having the relevant facts to hand. The latter requirement is a necessary condition of sound judgement since if an individual is ill informed on the issue under discussion, it is, if not certain, then highly likely that the corresponding judgement will be defective. This is as true of matters of moral and political moment as any other. To illustrate the point: if we are tempted to blame the Jews for being in some ways complicit in their annihilation because of their passivity in the face of the threat represented by the Nazis, a clear-headed appraisal of the reality of the situations that they confronted, up to and including the period of the so-called final solution, is imperative to make a justified assessment of the nature of the Jewish response to their plight. A nuanced appreciation of that plight will surely encourage a recognition of the inadequacy of talk of *the* Jewish response, will encourage a recognition that talk of passivity with its implications of simply accepting as inevitable what would happen whatever it was simply misrepresents the facts, and that in the limiting instance of the death camps the simply appalling nature of the circumstances in which they found themselves makes the notion of exercising choice barely feasible. It is in this last connection that Langer (1980) invokes the pregnant phrase of 'choiceless choices'. The facts as revealed by historical investigation make implausible any suggestion that seeks to blur the distinction between those who do evil and those who are the victims of it which talk of 'complicity' tends to foster. In an area in which we find ourselves confronting issues of the utmost significance for our understanding of ourselves and our possibilities, the importance of the facts seems undeniable.

I have dealt very quickly with a complex matter but the point is this: at the very heart of teaching about the Holocaust must be an accurate historical account of what as a matter of brute fact happened, and the seeking of perspectives that make sense of the facts. I do not suppose that making sense of the facts is uncontentious. It clearly is not. But teaching about the Holocaust must proceed on the basis of presenting it as an historical event with all that that entails. The story to be told will, as a matter of fact, be testimony to the role of prejudice, racism, discrimination and stereotyping in the shaping of human affairs. Exactly what was the role played by these manifestations of unreason in the unfolding story of the Nazi period is a matter of much debate. Was Hitler's virulent form of antisemitism the crucial determinant behind the story of the Holocaust or did the 'final solution' emerge more from the ad-hoc responses of bureaucrats to the changing circumstances in which they found themselves, such that the 'final solution' was only tenuously related to Hitler's racial and antisemitic fantasies? Wherever one stands on this notorious intentionalist–functionalist debate within Holocaust history, it is nevertheless common ground to recognize Hitler's racism as a factor in the story to be told. This period of history is replete with reminders of the pernicious effects of finding (unjustified) reasons to disregard the justified claims of other humans upon us.

The story to be told will certainly highlight how Germany used the resources of a modern state – its technological and bureaucratic resources – to implement in a way that was previously unimaginable, policies of genocide and social engineering. In this sense the Holocaust in a peculiarly modern phenomenon. It allows us more than a glimpse of what henceforth was all too possible. The story to be told will demonstrate only too graphically that apathy, indifference and silence in a society that had enjoyed democracy, and which was one of the great bastions of European culture and civilization, certainly made it much easier for the Nazis to perpetrate the horrors they inflicted upon the Jews and all the other non-Jews who in various ways were also the victims of the inhumanity that distinguished the Third Reich.

Teaching about the Holocaust as a historical phenomenon must be concerned with introducing students to historical method. It must also be concerned to get students to think in an historical manner. It must equip them with all the skills appropriate to studying the past. The acquisition of such competences is fundamental to that other task of making sense of what the Holocaust represents as a statement about humanity and of what we are capable. As stated previously, history provides the bedrock for informed discussion about the larger issues raised by the Holcaust. What a carefully wrought historical understanding will allow us to recognize is that racism, prejudice, antisemitism and other manifestations of discrimination enter into human affairs in all kinds of ways and with all manner of outcomes. We do not need to embrace the implausible claim that racism leads inevitably to genocide to determine that it is, in all of its manifestations, to be resisted. Any programme of moral or political education to be true to its nature and point must reinforce this determination.

Reflecting on the significance of the Holocaust

Studying the Holocaust must make us aware that discrimination, prejudice of certain kinds, racism and stereotyping have played a destructive role in human affairs; to utilize that heightened awareness in the construction of a more humane and compassionate society is another matter. To recognize others as centres of consciousness, to recognize that they have hopes and fears, have expectations of the future as do we, to recognize that they too can feel joy and suffering, is part of what it is to see another as a human being. It is a fundamental element (perhaps *the* fundamental element) of our received morality to see every human being as equally worthy of respect in recognition of their inherent dignity. A logical entailment of this commitment is that everyone's interests presumptively count as much as anyone else's. Why discrimination on the grounds of race, sex, ethnic grouping or cultural grouping offends so much against our basic ethic is that it denies proper standing to individuals as human beings by virtue of considerations that are irrelevant to how as humans they ought to be treated. What the Nazi years show is how fragile this disinterested ethic is, and how easily so many, not originally party to the violation of the claims of others, lent themselves to everything that followed in the wake of the breach of the ethic proclaiming the equality of human beings. Finding ways of resisting casts of mind, sentiments and outlooks that diminish our fellow humans now becomes a supremely urgent task. This task is made all the more urgent as we see only too well that all the conditions – more improved technologies of death and more efficient bureaucracies – making it easier to slaughter our fellow creatures are now an integral feature of our lives.

There is, however, a prior question that needs to be addressed. Is the key lesson of the Holocaust that we must give up on all hopes of the betterment of the human condition? Is the story of the Holocaust a reminder to us that it is the fate of human beings to endure? Should we (as Langer suggests) recognize 'the impotence of the humanistic vision in an age of atrocity' (Langer, 1980, p. 310)? If this is the lesson, all our programmes of education are without point before we start. In his passionate and persuasive work, Geras (1998, p. 129) accuses Langer (a much admired interpreter of the Holocaust) of reconstruing the accounts offered us by survivors of their experiences in such a way as to blot 'any saving chink of light which anyone else, including the survivor witnesses themselves, may have witnessed *for* themselves and brought back with them'. Langer's artifice is devoted to the one end of purveying darkness. Geras suggests (*idem*) that while in no way balancing out the moral darkness of the Holocaust, there is nevertheless as he puts it 'even in the very depths' evidence of another moral universe – a universe in which there is still affirmation of human solidarity, the effort to preserve dignity, of human sympathies. All evidence of what Geras describes as reaching 'towards a different past or better future' (*idem*). Coupled with the rejection of the facile proposition that humans reveal their essential nature in extreme situations, there is no reason to give up on the very idea of moral progress. We simply know better, and more realistically, how hard we have to fight for it.

CURRICULAR REFLECTIONS

Certain concerns arising out of our understanding of the Holocaust seem to be of central significance to any educational programme concerning itself with the Nazi years. They are issues that go to the very heart of both morality as an enterprise and democracy as a social practice. If there is a concern to reaffirm certain human decencies, discourage some ways of viewing our fellow humans, a desire to preserve the democratic temper of a society, persuade young people to accept responsibility, at both the individual and social level, for what is done in their names, some broad concerns must structure the detailed delivery of such programmes of Holocaust education.

A serious effort must be made to engage with the history of the Nazi period. This will embrace its origins, its unfolding stages with particular references to the treatment of the Jews over time culminating in the decision in early 1942 to embrace the 'final solution'. In all of this the treatment of all those other groups who suffered at the hands of the racialist and eugenic theories of the Nazis must receive due attention. Such a programme of study will provide the bedrock of fact upon which more refined judgements can be made, not only in respect of the events of the Holocaust themselves but also in respect of contemporary events (think of the too many crude judgements made about contemporary politics rooted in inadequate analogies with the Holocaust).

A serious effort must be made to reflect upon what the Holocaust might be able to tell us about the sustaining of our democracy – talk of democracy here going well beyond simple majority rule to that whole constellation of attitudes, moral principles, recognition and acceptance of individual rights which ideally inform the democratic way of life – and importantly related to this.

A serious effort must be made to confront the issues of moral responsibility, individual and collective, so starkly presented for our consideration by the Holocaust. What is moral indifference? Is it an endemic feature of modern societies? Are there ways we might combat it? Are there ways in which we can encourage a greater preparedness to aid our neighbour? Who is our neighbour? Can we rescue from the darkness of the Holocaust glimpses of hope for the future? All these questions are applicable to the behaviour of individuals and nation-states.

CONCLUSION

The detailed programmes for teaching about the Holocaust will be many and various. The wealth of historical detail arising from the study of the Holocaust, the explosion of literature surrounding the topic, the different contributions made by the different disciplines guarantee such an outcome. This book will reflect some of that diversity (see also Supple, 1993; Landau, 1998). This chapter will offer no thoughts on how best teaching about the Holocaust is likely to be delivered. Different areas of the curriculum can all make a vital contribution to the task. The whole gamut of teaching methods is potentially available to the skilled teacher. But any programme of Holocaust education has, I have suggested, got to be historically well informed and be driven by the desire to learn lessons from this greatest of abominations that can be incorporated into all of our lives and at all levels. Even without the Holocaust there would be good enough reasons to alert young people to the issues of discrimination in all of their manifold forms and of the need to recognize the claims of others upon us. The significance of the Holocaust is that it is the apotheosis of the tendencies of discrimination and a refusal to look out for our neighbour. But there was nothing inevitable about it. We have to believe that it could have been averted. Later chapters will say more on the pedagogical issues of teaching about the Holocaust. However it is done, I feel moved to say this: to leave students unmoved by the Holocaust, to have exposed students to the Holocaust and for them not to have felt the misery and degradation of the victims of Nazi ideological fantasies, is not to have done justice to the horrors constitutive of the Holocaust. Teaching about the Holocaust cannot be and must not be an intellectual exercise alone. The way to bring home the realities of the Holocaust is to confront students with its horrors and allow them a vision of a world bereft of moral concern. There is a literature – the testimony of the survivors – which allows us a glimpse of such a world. Think of the writings of Primo Levi, Charlotte Delbo, Terrence Des Pres, Jean Amery, Tadeusz Borowski and all those other writers and diarists who have given us an insight into the special hell they endured. In this area the conjoining of intellectual and emotional responses is peculiarly demanded. The purely intellectual apprehension of human beings as bearers of rights, as ends in themselves, as deserving of equality of dignity and respect comes to nothing unless we also recognize that others suffer just like us, can be hurt just like us. In short, there needs to exist a recognition of the common vulnerabilities of all humans. One of the tasks of moral education is to encourage a recognition of these shared propensities. Without taking a final view on the exact status of the moral principles to which our society characteristically appeals, it seems clear that commitment to the formal moral principles mentioned above will not be enough to generate the appropriate extension of sympathy to others. As Rorty suggests, 'Moral education ... is sentimental or nothing' (Rorty, 1998, p. 121). An education about the Holocaust, above all other things, simply must convey the misery and degradation that it brought in its wake. Holocaust survivors wrote so that we should understand the outrage to which they were subjected. We owe them no less than to ensure their voice is heard and the lessons learned. It is not the task of Holocaust educators to disguise from the young the depths to which humanity can sink. From such an appreciation may grow the determination to, individually and collectively, diminish the huge amount of human misery brought about by the moral indifference and sheer wickedness of other humans.

Holocaust education stands, of course, as an expression of our desire that never again should Jews be subject to similar barbarities. It also strives to offer us the hope that in the future no group will be exposed to like abominations on the grounds of race, religion or culture. However, the most cursory acquaintance with recent history suggests that the lessons to be learned from studying the Holocaust need endlessly to be brought to everyone's attention. The significance of teaching about the Holocaust as part of an educational programme can scarcely be overemphasized.

REFERENCES

Arendt, H. (1979) *Eichmann in Jerusalem: A Report on the Banality of Evil.* Harmondsworth: Penguin.

Geras, N. (1998) *The Contract of Mutual Indifference.* London: Verso.

Landau, R. (1998) *Studying the Holocaust.* London: Routledge.

Lang, B. (1990) *Act and Idea in the Nazi Genocide.* Chicago: University of Chicago Press.

Langer, L. (1980) The writer and the Holocaust experience. In H. Friedlander and S. Milton (eds) *The Holocaust: Ideology, Bureaucracy, and Genocide.* New York: Greenwood Press.

Magurshak, D. (1988) The incomprehensibility of the Holocaust: tightening up some loose usage. In A. Rosenberg and G.E. Myers (eds) *Echoes from the Holocaust.* Philadelphia, PA: Temple University Press.

Rorty, R. (1998) A defence of minimalist liberation. In A. Allen and M. Regan (eds) *Debating Democracy's Discontent.* New York: Oxford University Press, pp. 117–25.

Supple, C. (1992) *From Prejudice to Genocide: Learning about the Holocaust*. Stoke-on-Trent: Trentham Books.
Wiesenthal, S. (1976) *The Sunflower*. New York: Schocken Books.

Part 2

International Overviews

Chapter 5

Teaching the Holocaust in Germany

Hanns-Fred Rathenow
(Translation: Sabine Kussatz)

'Do German pupils learn about the Holocaust?' This is a question occasionally asked by foreign history teachers when they visit a memorial site for victims of National Socialism in Germany. It is a question which reveals the suspicion that German history lessons might take no account of the most difficult and for Germans most embarrassing chapter of their national history. Perhaps it is thought that, at best, German history lessons are restricted to minimal accounts that do not face the facts.

THE HOLOCAUST: PROBLEMS OF THE TERM

Before I can answer the question of how the Holocaust is taught in Germany, a definition of the term 'Holocaust' has to be given. In general, the term implies the murder of the European Jews by the Nazis, which was planned bureaucratically and carried out systematically as if on an assembly line. As a rule, this definition does not involve the genocide of Sinti and Roma ('Gypsies'), Slavs, whose fate was already announced in Hitler's *Mein Kampf*, or the systematic murder of people with disabilities, called euthanasia, which served as a test case for the extermination of other groups subject to racial discrimination. The Holocaust was unique because certain groups of people were declared to be 'subhuman creatures', so-called 'unworthy life'. These people were rigorously treated as objects whose murder was regarded as an industrial and bureaucratic problem. This was especially true following the Wannsee conference on 20 January 1942.

The widespread use of the term 'Holocaust' is directly related to its Old Testament meaning of 'burnt offering', which tends to exclude all non-Jewish victims of National Socialism. But German history lessons on the Holocaust include the Sinti and Roma, those with disabilities and the political enemies of the Nazis as well as the Jews. German pupils cannot escape dealing with the entire problem. Holocaust education in Germany is also more than just dealing with the victims of the Holocaust: it also includes an examination of the ideological basis of National Socialism, the social conditions that were the foundation of the Third Reich and the planning and course of the Second World War. Other terms which are sometimes used interchangeably with 'Holocaust' are 'Shoah' and 'Auschwitz'.

REUNIFICATION OF GERMANY

The situation in Germany after reunification is contradictory. On the one hand, there have been numerous right-wing attacks on foreigners, especially in eastern Germany where people felt socially insecure. On the other hand, there is a growing readiness in public to come to terms with the crimes of the German *Wehrmacht* (armed forces), who took an oath to Hitler, and the attitude of the so-called common people, the 'very normal' Germans. Since the end of the 1960s there has hardly been another example where Germany's recent past and its consequences have been so thoroughly discussed in public. In this respect Goldhagen's book (1996) and Victor Klemperer's (1998) *I Will Bear Witness* met a ready readership. The recent attention to Nazi crimes is not limited to Germany. It occurs in other countries, too, with different aspects being discussed. In France a lawsuit was brought against Papon. In Switzerland the relationship of the banks to the 'Nazi gold' is investigated. In the United States compensation claims of former forced labourers are negotiated and there is discussion as to whether the knowledge of the murder of the Jews, which the Allied governments had too, should have led to appropriate action. All these debates about Nazi crimes seem to have gained a new dimension. Even the Vatican has started to open new pages in its history more than 50 years after the end of Nazi rule. The former *Bundespräsident* Richard von Weizsäcker, in a speech on 8 May 1985, 40 years after the German capitulation, pointed out the changed situation that came with a new generation: 'The young are not responsible for what has happened, but they are responsible for what is made out of it [in history].'

HISTORICAL ASPECTS OF POST-WAR GERMANY: EAST GERMANY

Some experts in political socialization were startled when right-wing and neo-Nazi activities frequently occurred in the area of the former German Democratic Republic (GDR) after the political change in central Europe in 1989. It was believed that East German citizens had been immunized against racism and xenophobia by their 'anti-fascist' education. But there was already the potential for extreme right-wing activity in the GDR before 1989, which was officially referred to as 'hooliganism' despite the fact that prejudice against foreigners was made taboo as foreign workers (especially those from countries of the Eastern bloc and developing countries) came to live in the GDR as a result of international agreements. A large part of the population did not come into contact with these people, so that the new openness, part of which was absorbing asylum-seekers, undermined their sense of security. They reacted negatively or even with hostility to foreigners. Many young people in eastern Germany were undergoing identity crises caused by a high level of unemployment and economic and social instability. This led to a situation in which these young people preferred the right-wing DVU (Deutsche Volksunion) party in some places. In 1998 the DVU gained 13 per cent of the vote in Sachsen-Anhalt.

Ever since its foundation on 7 October 1949 the GDR considered itself to be the 'culmination of the revolutionary German labour movement' and the 'stronghold of anti-fascism'. After the Second World War, two groups of politicians took leading positions in the 'first worker's and farmer's state on German soil'. The first group consisted of Communist resistance fighters who were opposed to National Socialism. The second group included political exiles who were appointed to leading positions within the Soviet zone by the Soviet occupying power immediately after the war. The national government and the party leadership of the GDR named themselves as 'winners of history', because they had found the 'big industry' (*Großindustrie*) 'the junkerdom' and the 'armed forces' guilty of Nazi crimes. GDR politicians thought to have achieved their aim of 'extinguishing' the spirit of 'Nazism' and 'chauvinism' by completing the expropriation of the ownership of large estates and 'big business' only one year after the end of the war.

The idea of anti-fascism became the most important foundation for the social and political legitimacy of the GDR. It not only became the guideline for political speeches, party conference documents and slogans of everyday life in the GDR, but also determined the character of school legislation and the curricula in the schools of the GDR. The working class was exonerated from social guilt and moral responsibility for the Nazi crimes by crediting them with unlimited anti-fascist behaviour. There was no examination of individual biographies or breaks with history during the National Socialist era, as was done in West Germany during the late 1960s. The historical responsibility was imposed on the (West German) Federal Republic of Germany (FRG) which was considered to be the successor state of the Third Reich. Immediately after the war the Social Democratic Party (SPD) and the German Communist Party (KPD) turned to the German people and as the basis of democratic school reform, asserted that:

> The rising generation of the German people ... has to be free of Nazi and military thoughts; must be brought up with a new spirit, with a spirit of a fighting democracy and a spirit of friendship between the peace-loving peoples, brought up to an independent, upright, liberal and progressive thought and action. (Dokumente, 1970, p. 73)

Anti-fascism was the fundamental principle for raising children and for education at schools and in out-of-school activities like those of the Young Pioneers, the Free German Youth (FDJ) or the Society for Sports and Technique (GST). It ran through (each and) every (single) subject and grade and also had influence on the classes preparing 14-year-olds for the *Jugendweihe*, a ceremony in which the young people were given adult social status. It replaced the Christian confirmation almost completely. The 'German workers' heroic fight against oppression, war and fascism, led by the Communists accompanied the pupils all the way from primary school until they left school. The (historical) anti-fascist resistance was equated with Communist resistance alone. The model of the 'all-round educated socialist personality' did not exist to learn how to question authority, but to adapt to existing conditions. Criticism was allowed only if the norms of the system were not called into question. Sense of responsibility served the aim of getting the socialist and social norms generally accepted.

The 'heroism of the anti-fascist resistance fight' of Communist Party members who were incarcerated in concentration camps was especially emphasized in the national memorial sites (*Nationale Mahn- und Gedenkstätten*) at former concentration camps. Thus concentrating on the fate of political prisoners and the Communist-organized resistance during National Socialism, the Holocaust, was made a peripheral phenomenon. The hierarchy was very clear; Jehovah's witnesses, homosexuals or Sinti and Roma were made marginal and only Communist victims were referred to as 'victims of fascism'.

Although one of the basics of Nazi ideology, antisemitism was ignored in the historical research in the GDR. It started to become an object only in the 1960s when the leadership of the GDR had granted recognition to the few remaining Jewish communities. Towards the end of the 1980s, when it was seeking international recognition the relationship of the GDR to the history of the German Jews changed. History classes in schools corresponded to this development.

HISTORICAL ASPECTS OF POST-WAR GERMANY: WEST GERMANY

The recommendations of the American education committee in post-war Germany immediately after the end of the war stated that the best and only tool to achieve democracy was education. The resulting education policy of the Allies after the Second World War was referred to as 're-education'. Despite this programme the first period of examination of the crimes of the Third Reich only led to a de-politicization of political education up to the early 1960s. The 'German Education Committee' (*Deutscher Ausschuß für das Erziehungs- und Bildungswesen*) emphasized in its 1955 report on political education the necessity of political education, but had to admit difficulties in coming to terms with the past. Coming to terms with the past often meant remaining silent or suppressing the past. History books usually referred to 'Hitlerism', a concept suggesting that Hitler and his companions bore the main responsibility for the Nazi crimes while the German people itself was a victim of the terror and hardly knew anything about the crimes against humanity. In many places history lessons ended with the First World War or the end of the Weimar Republic. One reason for this was that many of the post-war teacher generation, most of whom were men at grammar schools, had participated in the war and therefore were often an active part of the system. The existence of supporters and accomplices was not considered because of the involvement of these people.

Around the end of 1959 large quantities of anti-semite graffiti in Cologne startled the public. Young people had scrawled swastikas all over a synagogue and on Jewish gravestones. On 30 January 1960, the 'German Education Committee' explained these anti-semitic excesses mainly by 'the parents' failure in bringing up their sons and daughters' and the 'weaknesses of German politics'. Accusations blaming school education were turned away as being too one-sided. The KMK, the Standing Conference of the Ministers of Education and Cultural Affairs of the *Länder* (states) reacted too. A short while later, they decided how student teachers should deal with the destruction of the rule of law under National Socialism.

The start of the Cold War reduced the influence of the American re-education policy on the German school system; fascism and Communism were often put on the same level and anti-Communism became the 'official civic attitude'. The case of Hermann Joseph Abs (born 1901) illustrates the political and social development following the war. Abs was one of the key figures of the administration of the Nazi gold, but after the war he was elected honorary chairman of the Deutsche Bank. During National Socialism his tasks included the 'Aryanization' of Jewish fortunes. This meant transferring stocks of Jewish accounts to the Reich Finance Ministry by the German banks. Even though the Deutsche Bank was liquidated and Abs was taken to court, the financial institution and its top manager, just like many other industrial companies, was able to rise like a phoenix from the ashes and find its place in the German economic miracle. In 1951 Abs became main negotiator of the Adenauer government and took part in the London debt agreement. He managed to keep demands from former forced labourers and concentration camp prisoners away from the post-war reparations and achieved a postponement of these questions until the signing of the peace treaty. The Deutsche Bank became Germany's biggest financial institution and Abs its honorary chairman. He died in 1994. In 1999, fifty years after the foundation of the FRG, history caught up with his case. In February 1999 German newspapers reported in detail on the role of the Deutsche Bank in the credits that enabled the concentration camp of Auschwitz to be built. They also reported on the building site of IG Farben where prisoners had to work until they died (*Vernichtung durch Arbeit*). And Hermann Josef Abs did not know anything about it during all those years?

Up to the mid-1960s the memory of National Socialism was usually suppressed. This is partly due to the fact that in the FRG part of the old elite were again or still men of position and authority. A social process of rethinking started with the Eichmann trial in Israel in 1961–2 and the Auschwitz trial in Frankfurt in 1963–5. It reached its peak with the student movement (1967–8). For the first time, the 'generation of the fathers' were officially and vociferously put before a political and moral tribunal and forced to face the reality of their guilt and responsibility.

This also found expression in the school curricula which now went into details about the Holocaust. There was a KMK recommendation in the early 1960s saying that history books should from then on contain an intensive examination of National Socialism. A new pedagogical approach developed, influenced by the New Left and its social science approach, and following the Critical Theory of the *Frankfurter Schule*. The goals of this new approach concentrated on 'emancipation'. In history classes teachers used sociological and structural analyses of fascism, but they soon had to realize that these were not comprehended by the pupils.

The success of the American TV series *Holocaust* (1979) marked the beginning of a new epoch of school examination of National Socialism. Cognitive and effective ways of learning were connected by linking scientific analyses with the circumstances of the ordinary people, the contemplation of 'history from beneath' (*Geschichte von unten*) and the people's everyday life experiences during National Socialism. The emphasis on events of local history ('Dig where you are standing') and biographical approaches (eyewitnesses) led to a number of programmatic approaches in historical and political classes that are still fruitful now.

PRINCIPLES OF HISTORICAL AND POLITICAL EDUCATION IN GERMANY

Even before the end of the Nazi regime in May 1945, the four Allies had reached agreement on the future order in Germany; there should not be any centralist power structures. Therefore, in the Potsdam Agreement of 1945, the victorious powers apart from France agreed on decentralizing the political structures in favour of regional autonomy. When the FRG was founded it meant the creation of a federation consisting of the Federal government and the *Länder*. This was written down in the *Grundgesetz*, the German constitution, which was proclaimed on 23 May 1949. Hence Germany is a federal state like the United States. Article 70 of the *Grundgesetz* prescribes the competence which the Federal government (*Bund*) and the *Länder* have. For example, each of the sixteen *Länder* is responsible for its education system; this is called *Kulturhoheit der Länder* (independence in cultural and educational matters). As a result there are now – after the political change in 1989–90 – sixteen different statutes concerning the education system and thus sixteen different curricula for historical and political education (including such subjects as history, political studies and social studies). This is in contrast to France, England and Wales (national curriculum) or the former GDR ('democratic centralism'). But the *Länder* co-operate through the Standing Conference of the Ministers of Education and Cultural Affairs of the *Länder*, which was founded in 1948. One of the KMK's tasks is to ensure recognition of school-leaving qualifications within the *Bund*.

CURRICULA, AIMS AND CONTENT

The different curricula were much influenced by the political development in the individual *Länder* after the Second World War and thus affect historical and political classes differently. This covers guidelines concerning aims, volume of lessons and class contents. Curricula are like decrees of the superior authority which provide a framework, but give teachers space to act according to their own insights.

In any case, lessons about National Socialism are connected with teaching about fundamental democratic values as they are contained in the first articles of the *Grundgesetz*. These relate to English declarations of human rights of the seventeenth century, the constitution of the United States and the French *déclaration des droits de l'homme* of the closing years of the eighteenth century. Even though the *Länder* have cultural and educational autonomy the federal constitution (*Grundgesetz*) regulates the basics of educational work. This is done by the principle that federal law has precedence over the law of the *Land* (Article 31 of the *Grundgesetz*), for example Article 7 of the *Grundgesetz* states that the school system as a whole is under state supervision.

Paragraph 1 of the Berlin Education Act (Berliner Recht für Schule und Lehrer 1996, pp. 2000–3) goes back to the period immediately after the war, and includes elements of the Allied re-education approach. It makes clear what is now undisputed in the other *Länder* too:

> The aim has to be the creation of personalities that are able to oppose the ideology of National Socialism and other political ideologies which strive for tyranny. They have to be able to arrange state and social life on the basis of democracy, peace and human dignity. These personalities have to be

conscious of their responsibility for the general public and their attitude must be determined to recognize the basic equality of any human being, respect any honest conviction and recognize the necessity for a progressive arrangement of social conditions and a peaceful understanding between the peoples.

The KMK has an effect on the education work of the *Länder* through its recommendations. In recent decades there have been also quite a few recommendations dealing with the treatment of National Socialism in the school curriculum. On the occasion of a meeting on 28–29 September 1995 the KMK stated in Halle upon Saale:

National Socialism abused national and social ideas and broke radically and programmatically with democratic traditions. Its criminal politics led to the catastrophe of the Second World War and the Holocaust. This resulted in Germany being partitioned for more than forty years. It is the duty of school to familiarize pupils with the main developments of Germany's history and pay special attention to continuities and breaks in its recent history in particular.

In connection with the topic 'The *Grundgesetz* as a normative aid to orientation for the inner reunification' the KMK expects the young to concern themselves with and identify with the principles and values of the *Grundgesetz*. Special attention has to be given to acceptance of the idea that no negative experience of democracy ever justifies violence or totalitarian action as a means of solving conflicts. These recommendations of the KMK have their counterpart in the curricula for historical and political education in the *Länder*. Furthermore there are decrees issued by the cultural ministries, for example at the beginning of 1996 the KMK decided to leave the arrangements of the commemoration day for the victims of National Socialism (27 January, the day of the liberation of Auschwitz) to the *Länder* and to individual schools so that there were no guidelines on federal level.

The examination of the recent past during history and politics classes usually provides for a visit to a nearby memorial site for the victims of National Socialism. One example of how this local history approach is implemented is the 1991 Hamburg curriculum for politics and history in comprehensive schools. It suggests that while dealing with the topic pupils should visit one of the following memorial sites:

• the memorial site Neuengamme (memorial itself, buildings, house of documents)
• memorial of the city of Hamburg for the victims of the Nazi

persecution and *Totenmal* for the Hamburg bomb victims in the Ohlsdorfer cemetery
● memorial for the children of Bullenhuser Damm
● examination of the memorial for the infantry regiment no. 76 (1936) and the memorial at the Dammtorbahnhof created by Alfred Hrdlicka.

The Hamburg curriculum thus realizes the idea of the maxim 'Dig where you are standing'. The teaching unit 'German Fascism and the Second World War' for classes 9 and 10 includes the methodological suggestions above. Main focuses of this teaching unit are the persecution of the Jews, the extermination of Slavs, Gypsies, mentally disabled people and homosexuals, resistance against the Nazi dictatorship and the Hitler Youth, as an example of everyday life in Nazi Germany.

In the past the KMK often gave its view on the treatment of National Socialism at school. In 1978 it stated that an important task of the school is 'to enable pupils to judge competently and to support this by supplying them with solid knowledge, especially about Germany's recent history' (KMK resolution from 20 April 1978). This is also true for decrees enacted by the cultural ministries which are often made because of current events and influence the planning of history and politics lessons. In 1989, the Bremen senator for education and science, for example, referring to a debate in the Bremen parliament on growing right-wing extremism, asked all teachers to conduct memorial site trips and teach this topic within the bounds of the debates about fascism, neo-fascism and xenophobia. Pupils in Bremen are supposed to visit a memorial site for concentration camp victims at least once during their school days. Similar recommendations are expressed by numerous other *Länder*. All *Länder* accompany these recommendations by offers of further education for teachers.

The ideas of what pupils should learn in history and politics classes in the sixteen *Länder* do not differ very much in relation to National Socialism and the Holocaust. All sixteen curricula describe the topic 'National Socialism and the Second World War' with the keywords 'concentration camps', 'extermination camp' and 'Holocaust', compulsory for the ninth and tenth grades. On average there are twenty periods a week available in *Sekundarstufe I* (11/13 to 16 years) for this topic. In *Sekundarstufe II* (17–19 years), including vocational schools and schools where the *Abitur* (A levels) can be obtained, like grammar schools, the topic of National Socialism is once again taken up and deepened, for example in comparison to other totalitarian systems of government. Often the curricula draw attention to possibilities of cross-curricular approaches and other integrating methods. Subjects involved include biology, ethics, religious education, music or German. Some *Länder* (for example, Berlin and Lower Saxony) go into the question of individual fates during National Socialism even earlier; they take up this topic in primary school or the so-called *Förderstufe* (11/12 years – a phase of mixed-ability teaching intended to reveal the aptitudes and abilities of individual pupils). The cultural minister of Lower Saxony suggests that there is a need to proceed sensitively and in a manner appropriate to the pupils' ages when dealing with the topic 'Children and young people at the Nazi time' in the subject *Welt- und Umweltkunde* (world studies). The minister further suggests that pupils examine regional events. (Niedersächsisches Kultusministerium, 1992, p. 20). The Berlin curriculum for the fifth and sixth grades proposes the following topics: 'Hitler establishes a dictatorship and persecutes its enemies', 'Persecution of the Jews, the SS and concentration camps' and 'May 1945 Germany in ruins'.

METHODS OF TEACHING THE HOLOCAUST

'The demand that Auschwitz must never happen again is the most crucial education. It is so much more important than anything else that I don't feel I have to or should justify it.' This quotation is taken from a speech made by Theodor Adorno broadcast on radio in 1966 (Adorno, 1967, p. 111). The speech, entitled *Education After Auschwitz*, starts with this quotation. His position, presented twenty years after the liberation from Hitler's fascism, is still valid now.

History and political lessons about Auschwitz must not aim at producing consternation in pupils: this is not education. Making pupils feel upset comes close to manipulation and indoctrination. There is a great danger that an excessive amount of shared suffering might lead to internal repression and impotence. Yet Holocaust education cannot be done without talking about the feelings of other people's distressing and painful experiences. Moreover one fundamental educational task is to develop the ability to recognize one's own feelings and to talk about them with others.

Hartmut von Hentig (1993), the doyen of German post-war educationists, criticized the school system because it lets pupils leave school rich in knowledge but poor in experience, disorientated, dependent on other people and without any effective relationship with the community. This critique can easily be transferred to many areas of history and political education. Therefore each encounter between young people and the facts of National Socialism should be based on the question 'What has history to do with me?' The background to this question is that history is not just the past but a part of the present. What is taught to pupils as fact must not be presented to them as being the result of objective scientific endeavours, but as attempts to reconstruct and interpret past events by people with certain opinions about the events. Therefore, memorial sites, for example, reflect how a later generation interprets historical places. They are attempts to reconstruct past events in order to put them into a wider perspective. Concentration camp memorial sites are not to be mistaken for concentration camps: they have to be interpreted. For example, at Buchenwald the camp itself was changed by the Americans soon after the liberation. The GDR government then further imposed its own interpretation on the site and after 1990 a 'West' German view was dominant on the site. It is vital that students should understand these sorts of processes.

Abram and Heyl (1996) indicated that one should not solely concentrate on the extreme cruelties of National Socialism because this loses the impact of 'lesser' horrors of the Nazi system. The horror of the system is demonstrated by the numerous 'small cruelties', as Klemperer (1998) describes them in his diaries. Understanding this can promote empathy for victims as well as for culprits and other groups involved, like bystanders, helpers or people who resisted the system.

The question of how the Holocaust should be taught is asked again and again partly because of its growing distance from the present. Holocaust education is running out of eyewitnesses from the Nazi era. Victims and culprits, helpers and supporters, accomplices and contemporaries are dying out. So we have no direct link to the past. There is also, unfortunately, a growing emphasis on methods that trivialize the subject matter such as ticking boxes on clipboards.

Holocaust education should be based on Martin Buber's dialogic principle, which includes the demand for equal discussions. This is also referred to as symmetrical communication between teachers and students. There are no losers or winners. Teachers are participants in the conversation and thus learners themselves without dominating the conversation by their knowledge or age. This constitutes the difference between the traditional instructor and the facilitator. Stressing the dialogic principle in class implies cultivating patience in difficult situations, for example in a discussion where pupils are denying the Holocaust. Teachers frequently say that the only way to meet right-wing provocations is to ignore them or dismiss them as anti-Semitic neo-Nazi propaganda. The attitude that leads to a denial of the Holocaust will rarely be challenged by facts or matter-of-fact arguments, but nevertheless it is important not to turn individuals into victims or substitute the teacher's authenticity with structural violence. Young people like to get attention and shouting 'Sieg Heil' in a market square, or refusing to talk about the Holocaust in class, is one way to get it.

Many German teachers prefer memorial site visits to textbook work. This is because the experience is more direct and it is possible to combine the sensations provoked by reality with the knowledge learnt at school. Even though this approach is very understandable, there is the danger that the reality of a memorial site leads to 'blind' opinions. Kant referred to this point by saying that terms without an image are empty and opinions without terms are blind. Another danger, especially when visiting concentration camp memorial sites, is that exhibited memories are mistaken for historical facts so that inner impressions coming from an exhibition might be taken for reality. It is the teacher's task to uncover and arrange the different layers and levels that have deposited on concentration camps, synagogues or other historical places over the decades. These layers and levels restrict the range of interpretations, especially in concentration camps, where interpretations have to be done by the visitors.

CONCLUSION

Holocaust education is not about preserving Nazi horror but about learning from history to provide the basis of hope for the future. Teachers must help their students (in the words of the famous poem quoted in full at the end of Chapter 10 by Terry Haydn) to become more human. This is a vital task.

REFERENCES AND SUGGESTIONS FOR FURTHER READING

Abram, I. and Heyl, M. (1996) *Thema: Holocaust. Ein Buch für die Schule.* Reinbek: Rowohlt.

Adorno, T.W. (1967) Erziehung nach Auschwitz. In H.-J. Heydorn *et al.* (eds) *Zum Bildungsbegriff der Gegenwart.* Frankfurt/M.: Diesterweg.

Dokumente zur Geschichte des Schulwesens in der Deutschen Demokratischen Republik. Teil I: 1945–1955 (1970) Ausgewählt von Gottfried Uhlig. Berlin: Volk und Wissen (Monumenta Paedagogica, Bd. VI).

Goldhagen, D.J. (1996) *Hitler's Willing Executioners: Ordinary Germans and the Holocaust*. London: Little, Brown.
Hentig, H. von (1993) *Die Schule neu denken*. Munich: Hanser.
Klemperer, V. (1998) *I Will Bear Witness: The Diaries of Victor Klemperer*. New York: Random House.

Chapter 6

The Education Centre at the Auschwitz-Birkenau Memorial and Museum

Krystyna Oleksy

Theodor Adorno said that the words 'Auschwitz cannot be allowed to happen again' should be the goal of all education. Adorno's call seems more relevant now than ever before. The slogans of nationalism, intolerance, xenophobia and antisemitism have gained adherents all over Europe in recent years. This has occurred in Poland, too. Racist and nationalist violence are no longer confined to the margins of society. The very young are increasingly vulnerable. The 1990s have seen a wave of extremist demonstrations, arson, pogroms and aggression directed against foreigners. This phenomenon shows how quickly, and on how wide a scale, racial and anti-Semitic prejudices can turn into violence.

In Polish schools, the Holocaust is commonly taught as part of the history of the Second World War and the Nazi occupation. The subject is traditionally included in history and Polish lessons in the eighth grade, for students aged 15, and in the last year of secondary school. For many years, these lessons have been accompanied by trips to the Auschwitz-Birkenau Memorial and Museum.

Auschwitz is a symbol of evil, of the hatred and contempt engendered in interpersonal relations and of the violence and oppression engendered in society by racism and a lack of respect for other peoples. This place should therefore be an educational centre. It should be a place where the best specialists co-operate to develop new educational methods, and where Polish and foreign teachers can find help, practical advice and a wide range of methodological support. Questions about the place of the individual in society must be asked within the context of the history of the Auschwitz concentration camp: what is our relationship to the world around us, and above all to other people? What are we capable of? People caught up in the labyrinth of social conditions and relations often forget about such moral problems. Auschwitz is a place that can often remind us in the most tangible of ways that the moral order around us is fragile. In this place where history is frozen at one of its most chilling moments, we may remember how necessary it is to keep trying to perfect and reinforce that moral order.

As a historical fact, Auschwitz teaches us about the institutional forms of community life that can lead to genocide. As a moral experience, Auschwitz shows us the interpersonal relations, emotional states and states of consciousness that made possible bureaucratized cruelty and the murder of defenceless, innocent human beings. As long as Auschwitz prompts the living to reflect on the fate of those who were murdered here, it will be needed as an enduring challenge to the human conscience and awareness. As long as this remains true, it will serve as more than merely a cemetery and a melancholy place of remembrance.

All over the world, there has been a growth of interest in Auschwitz. In many countries, special centres have been founded to prepare teachers and students to confront the history of Auschwitz and other Nazi death camps where the destruction of the Jews was carried out during the Second World War. The fact that the Nazis built these camps in occupied Poland compelled the country to become a centre for such studies. Auschwitz is a symbol throughout the world. The Auschwitz Memorial and Museum must necessarily function as a significant centre for education about the history of the camp, about the Holocaust and about the history of the Jews in Poland. The museum co-operates with other centres in these fields, but the inadequacy of the available resources has so far blocked the realization of many plans and initiatives.

From its founding, the museum has engaged in forward-looking educational activities aimed at young people and designed to ensure that this tragic part of the past can never be repeated. However, remembrance was the main task for the people who established the museum in 1947. The suffering and death of those people who were killed in the gas chambers immediately after arriving at Auschwitz were commemorated, as were the suffering and death of those who fell victim to the inhuman conditions of camp existence. The former prisoners thus understood their task in relation to the tragic fate of the dead.

The first visitors to the newly liberated camp were well aware, from personal experience, of the horrors of the occupation and the war. They knew who the victims were and who the perpetrators were. It seems justifiable to say that the first post-war generations of Poles and people from other countries that had been occupied by the Nazis had a broad fund of such knowledge. Those who were born soon after the war learned about such things directly from their parents. For all these people Auschwitz was, and still is, first of all a cemetery and place of remembrance, and only second a place of education and study.

The young people who now visit Auschwitz, however, were born decades after the end of the Second World War. Auschwitz has different meanings for them, depending on their national, social and religious backgrounds. Some have a very personal attitude, while others display indifference and distance themselves from the history of Auschwitz. The starting point for educational work with young people is identifying their attitude. From there, it is possible to acquaint them with the history of the camp, and to point out the political, social, historical and psychological processes and mechanisms that led to Auschwitz. Young people should know that Auschwitz was the work of ordinary people who were often similar to us. They were ordinary people before the rise of Nazism, and after the fall of Nazism. Nothing marked them as different from their neighbours, as was repeatedly demonstrated in the trials of the war criminals. Presenting the perpetrators as monsters or sadists would be the best way to tear Auschwitz out of its historical context and to reject any personal responsibility for what could happen in the future. Our task is to show how, given certain circumstances, people can condone cruelty and follow immoral, inhuman orders. Such a presentation makes the problem relevant and prevents it from being regarded as remote history.

It is impossible to imagine the inhuman conditions in which people in the camp had to fight for survival at the biological level. Yet the fact that these conditions were established by ordinary people for other ordinary people must be an occasion for reflection. It seems imperative to ask: what would my fate have been in those times? If we pose the question honestly, there are no unambiguous answers. In my opinion, the most important thing is the very posing of the question. It forces us to take the sides of both the victims and the perpetrators. People have no right to assume that they would be heroic or evil –

especially when they bear in mind how easy it is to yield to pressures incomparably less severe than the pressures to which people on both sides of the barbed wire fence were subjected.

Auschwitz offers many positive examples of the way that people can maintain their moral autonomy and maintain their humanity, even in such inhumane a setting as a concentration camp. Two educational approaches are possible. The first emphasizes such exceptional figures in the history of Auschwitz as Father Kolbe, Captain Pilecki and Róza Robota. This approach presents these figures as moral models, and suggests that even people who are weak and vulnerable to pressure can be capable of active resistance. Such outstanding examples of fellowship, solidarity and resistance can be sources of hope and optimism, and proof that resistance is possible in any predicament. The prevailing approach, however, should aim at convincing young people that they have a duty to learn about the world and the mechanisms and circumstances that govern the world, in order to try to prevent danger. We should realize that political and social relations depend on our actions. We should be aware that passivity or ignoring simple or simplistic explanations for conflicts can lead to horrific results, for which we, too, will be responsible.

Reflection on what happened at Auschwitz concentration camp should also show that what happened there was a result of the fact that people were treated as objects. Prisoners were deprived of their identities, rights and morality. They were reduced to the status of instruments to be exploited. In the light of such an interpretation, every instance of exploitation, of treating people in an instrumental way, becomes a step in the direction of Auschwitz. Such an awareness should lead to an attitude of responsibility for others and for oneself. It should also teach self-criticism and self-control.

Auschwitz means many things. Above all, it is the largest cemetery in the history of humanity. Each trip to Auschwitz should be a sort of pilgrimage. Paying one's respects to the victims and recognizing their suffering are fundamental conditions of being at Auschwitz. An awakened conscience, sympathy and imagination are necessary for further educational work.

The fact that Auschwitz has become a universal symbol in the world places a grave educational responsibility on the memorial and museum. That is why the Education Centre was established: its tasks include training teachers and students alike. It makes use of the latest advances in the disciplines of education, sociology, psychology, history and theology. Specialized programmes are prepared for various groups, in consultation with sociologists and anthropologists. These programmes enable adults, as well as young people, to understand two fundamental issues. First, how was it possible for Auschwitz to happen in the middle of the twentieth century? Second, who planned, built and ran the camp, who were the victims, and why were they sent to Auschwitz? In both cases, it is necessary that the search for answers be based on concrete people whose names are known.

As mentioned above, the young people who visit Auschwitz now were born decades after the end of the Second World War. The place they come from determines what Auschwitz means to them. In some cases, we encounter a deep personal attitude toward the camp. In other cases, the concentration camp seems as distant as the Middle Ages. This is the starting point for the first educational task of acquainting the young visitors with the history of the camp.

It can be very difficult to strike a balance between history and the present. Providing information is a crucial task. The issues connected with Auschwitz, after all, are not matters of faith, but rather of knowledge. It is necessary to state unambiguously what happened here, and who did what to whom – to say who the perpetrators were and who the victims were. I would like to emphasize that, even though the complicated moral and philosophical problems involved are universal, it is unthinkable not to say who the perpetrators and the victims were. Silence in this regard would look like manipulation or an effort to efface responsibility or to conceal the identity of the victims. This is particularly important in the case of the Jews, the Poles and the Roma.

Young people from Poland and other countries are often unable to relate to their own lives the information that 90 per cent of the victims of Auschwitz were Jewish. In Poland and in some other countries, there was no revival of Jewish life after the Holocaust. It is therefore necessary to illustrate Jewish life using specific examples, from specific towns and villages. It is necessary to help young people to understand that the Holocaust was not only a terrible crime and a tragedy for the Jewish people, but also an irreversible loss for Poland. It meant the end of an epoch, of something that can never be recovered.

In the light of everything that has been said above, the Education Centre at the Auschwitz Memorial and Museum has developed programmes to help teachers and students to prepare for visits. There are programmes for short stays and for study residencies lasting several days. Almost half of the visitors to the museum are Polish students. We therefore place special emphasis on preparing aids for Polish teachers. In co-operation with the Pedagogical School in Cracow, we have prepared a postgraduate programme entitled

Totalitarianism, Nazism and the Holocaust, which includes a variety of issues connected with contemporary history, the history of the Jews and Polish–Jewish relations. Some of the subjects include:

- The Nazi movement and Nazi rule in Germany and occupied Europe
- The history and culture of the Jewish people before 1939
- Nazi concentration camps, with specific emphasis on Auschwitz concentration camp
- The persecution and destruction of the Jewish people under Nazi rule
- Poles and Jews during the Second World War and in the post-war period
- The Holocaust and concentration camps in literature and art
- The Holocaust and concentration camps in feature films and documentaries
- The Jewish people after the war
- After Auschwitz and the Holocaust: overcoming inter-group prejudices and the past; inter-faith dialogue
- Totalitarianism, Nazism and the Holocaust at school.

There is enormous interest in this programme. Teachers report that it fills a gap in their professional education and prepares them to take up these issues during their lessons.

Another form of support for teachers and the leaders of visiting groups consists of seminars and lecture programmes lasting several days, on the fate of specific ethnic and religious groups in Auschwitz concentration camp. The seminars include specialist tours of the former camp, screenings of films and documentaries, and work in the archives and art collections. Meetings with former prisoners are also featured frequently. Methodological workshops are devoted to the study of original source materials. Each participant receives a set of historical and methodological materials that can later be used as resources for independent study or as aids in preparing groups of young people for visits to Auschwitz. The museum also offers opportunities to use thematic sets of course materials (copies of original documents from the camp, eyewitness accounts and articles on specific issues). The documentation also includes archival photographs and works of art created by former prisoners while they were in the camp, or after liberation. These sets of materials cover the following themes:

- Poles in Auschwitz concentration camp
- Jews in Auschwitz concentration camp

- Roma in Auschwitz concentration camp
- Women in Auschwitz concentration camp
- Children in Auschwitz concentration camp
- The camp infirmary
- The prisoners' resistance and self-help movement
- Criminal experiments by physicians at Auschwitz
- The Romeo and Juliet of Auschwitz: eyewitness accounts of Edek Galiñski and Mala Zimetbaum.

People from Poland and other countries take part in the seminars prepared by the Education Centre. The subjects are defined in advance in co-operation with the organizers, or in line with requests from participants. Subjects have included:

- Auschwitz: history and symbolism
- Auschwitz and the city of Oświęcim: past and present
- The modern history and experience of the Jews of eastern Europe
- The Holocaust and contemporary forms of ethnic and religious prejudice.

The philosophical and moral issues connected with Auschwitz concentration camp are varied and complex. Nevertheless I believe that the most essential equipment for a visit to Auschwitz is knowledge. Seminar participants often ask us how to prepare young people for this challenging confrontation. I believe that the emphasis should be on conveying information, so that the visitors know exactly where they are going. The emotions will come in any case. Auschwitz is probably the most emotionally charged place on earth. The emotions arise spontaneously, and in a way that is often unpredictable. It is often very difficult to preserve the equilibrium between *emotio* and *ratio*. Sometimes, indeed, such a balance is impossible in a single visit. Yet the absence of either of these elements calls the sense of a visit into question. Young people who wish to learn something from history must begin with an exact knowledge of that history. They must be familiar with the mechanisms that set a chain of events in motion. Only then can they attempt a deep analysis of those events. Yet an intellectual approach is insufficient by itself. Empathy is also necessary; it provides the motivation for the continual broadening of knowledge. The emotions that occur during a visit are often a problem for those who feel them: they do not expect that the emotions will be so large or so intense. They sometimes feel lost and disoriented: they look at us adults in the hope that we will help them to find a way of expressing what they feel. At the same time, they fear that their behaviour will fall short of our expectations. They are sometimes convinced that they should display a certain facial expression at places like the death wall or the gas chamber.

The seminars organized by the museum are intended to help teachers deal with these difficult problems. Many of them later decide to return with their students for a longer study residency. Aside from a specialized, two-day tour of the camp terrain, these seminars also include lessons in the Archives and visits to exhibitions of camp art. Some groups decide to devote a dozen or more hours to physical labour connected with the maintenance of the grounds. This work is organized by the museum, which employs special leaders for such tasks. Many decades of experience have shown that such labour has a unique educational effect. Over the past few years, young people have worked at clearing the roads at Birkenau of the grass, soil and bushes that have appeared there since the war. This has led to the discovery of the original camp streets laid out by prisoner labour details between 1942 and 1944. Various objects dating from the time that the camp was in operation have been discovered during such work. These include personal effects of persons deported to Auschwitz. As they talk with each other and with their teachers, the young people discover a new, previously unknown dimension of Birkenau.

Other forms of Holocaust education offered by the museum's Education Centre include film symposia and museum lessons. Selected lesson subjects include:

- Life in Auschwitz concentration camp, as illustrated by profiles of selected prisoners
- Attitudes and behaviour in the camp
- SS Man, Capo, prisoner
- Auschwitz themes in film
- Memoir literature as a source of knowledge about Auschwitz concentration camp.

There is great interest in the offerings of the Education Centre among school and university students, as well as among teachers. Visitors are often unaware of what a large and complicated institution the museum is. I would therefore like to include some basic information about our collections and the various forms of work we carry out in the hope that this information will prove useful in planning a visit to Auschwitz. Among the offerings, there will be choices appropriate to the level of a given class, and to the requirements of the teacher.

THE AUSCHWITZ-BIRKENAU MEMORIAL AND MUSEUM OŚWIĘCIM, POLAND: GENERAL DESCRIPTION

An Act for establishing a museum on the grounds of the former Auschwitz camp was introduced by former prisoner Alfred Fiderkiewicz at a session of the Polish National Council on 31 December 1945. On 2 July 1947, the Polish Sejm approved an act for creating the Auschwitz-Birkenau State Museum on part of the grounds of the former Auschwitz I and Auschwitz II-Birkenau camps.The final boundaries of the museum were fixed in 1957.

The museum covers a total of 191 hectares: 20 hectares at Auschwitz I and 171 at Birkenau (including 20 hectares of forest). The museum grounds contain:

- 154 original camp buildings – 56 at Auschwitz I and 98 at Birkenau
- 300 ruins, including gas chambers and crematoria, barracks and other original camp buildings
- 13,844 metres of original camp fence – 2080 metres at Auschwitz I and 11,764 metres at Birkenau
- 10,955 metres of surfaced roads – 2595 meters at Auschwitz I and 8360 metres at Birkenau
- 2200 metres of railway track.

In 1962, a buffer zone was established around the museum grounds at Birkenau. A similar zone was established around the museum grounds at the site of Auschwitz I in 1977. The purpose of establishing a buffer zone was to preserve the authentic context of the site of martyrdom and to protect the original vestiges of the camp lying outside the boundaries of the museum. In 1979, the former grounds of Auschwitz concentration camp were inscribed in the Unesco registry of the World Cultural Heritage. (The proposal, written by the Polish Ministry of Culture and Art and its Department of Museums and Landmark Preservation, was sent to the secretariat of the World Heritage Committee, 7 Place de Fontenoy, Paris 75700, on 6 June 1978. The inscription was performed during the Third Session of the World Heritage Committee, which was held in Luxor 22–26 October 1979.)

The first exhibition was opened in original camp blocks on the Auschwitz I grounds in 1947. Expanded in 1950, it depicted the story of mass murder and the conditions to which prisoners were subjected in the camp. New exhibitions were opened in Blocks 4, 5, 6, 7 and 11 in 1955. These exhibitions, with some changes and additions, are still open to visitors. National exhibitions, established on the initiative of former prisoners from various countries who were organized under the auspices of the International Auschwitz Committee, have been opened in some original camp blocks since 1960. They primarily depict the fate of citizens of the countries from which the Nazis deported people to Auschwitz concentration camp.

No exhibitions have been established on the former grounds of the Birkenau camp, in view of the exceptional nature of the site – which is above all a cemetery – and also in view of the rudimentary nature of the original barracks preserved there. The one large-scale new element introduced at Birkenau is the International Monument to the Camp Victims, ceremonially unveiled in 1967. Work carried out by the museum in recent years has concentrated on elucidating and commemorating the grounds and buildings and highlighting significant places and events connected with the history of Auschwitz concentration camp.

Since Birkenau is regarded as the most important part of the camp complex, all working concepts and projects have begun in that section of the museum. New commemorative and explanatory plaques have been placed there. Further projects are underway. These are connected with areas outside the boundaries of the museum, including the *Judenrampe* and the road along which thousands of deportees walked from the unloading dock to Birkenau. In 1999 work was underway on new signs on the Auschwitz I grounds, in areas adjacent to those grounds and at the site of the Buna sub-camp.

The Auschwitz-Birkenau museum is required by law to collect, preserve and conserve the collections and buildings of the museum, to conduct research upon them and to make them accessible to visitors and to all people from Poland and the rest of the world.

ARCHIVES, PHOTOGRAPHIC STUDIO, FILM COLLECTION AND FORMER PRISONERS' INFORMATION BUREAU

The archive collections include original German camp documents, copies of documents obtained from other institutions in Poland and abroad, materials from the trials of Nazi war criminals, source materials dating from after the war (memoirs and eyewitness accounts by former prisoners and others), photographs, microfilms, photographic negatives, documentary and archival films, research stories, reviews, lectures, film and exhibition scripts, and research surveys.

The Archives have a Computer Department which is engaged in creating databases about the archival resources. At present, the collections include:

- 39,000 photographic negatives of camp prisoners
- more than 30,000 other negatives including photographs of the selection of Jews deported to Auschwitz from Hungary, the grounds and buildings of the camp when it was in operation and after liberation, photographs of civilian prisoners and their families, Resistance Movement photographs and other photographs
- 2426 photographs from civilian life, brought to the camp by deportees
- 720,375 microfilm frames
- more than 300 video cassettes (400 titles) containing films, reports, etc.
- 128 feature and documentary film titles
- 439 audiotapes of eyewitness accounts and memoirs and 1526 recorded accounts on deposit from the Provincial Museum in Katowice
- 134 volumes in the Testimonies collection, including more than 3000 accounts
- 200 volumes in the Memoirs collection, including more than 1000 memoirs
- 8952 camp letters
- 41 volumes of materials concerning the Resistance Movement in the camp and in adjacent areas
- 46 volumes of the Death Book, containing 69,000 death certificates of prisoners who died or were murdered in Auschwitz concentration camp
- 76 volumes of the records of the trials of Rudolf Hess and the Auschwitz camp garrison
- 248 volumes of documents from the Waffen SS and Police Central Building Authority in Auschwitz, containing technical documentation and blueprints for the construction and expansion of the camp and its infrastructure.

COLLECTIONS DEPARTMENT

The Collections Department primarily collects original camp objects, property stolen from deportees and found on the camp grounds, camp equipment and instruments of torture. The department also collects art objects, including paintings, prints, drawings, sculpture, decorative art, coins, medals, and posters on camp themes. The historical collections include:

- more than 90,000 items of property of murdered victims, such as shoes, luggage, brushes, Jewish prayer garments, prison uniforms, glasses and artificial limbs
- approximately 80 cubic metres of victims' shoes and metal articles found in the grounds of the Kanada II camp warehouses
- approximately 2000 kilograms of hair shorn from the victims of Auschwitz concentration camp
- 2500 kilograms of various metal objects, including umbrella parts, razors, buttons, and so on.

The artistic collections include more than 6000 paintings, sculptures and prints created in the camp or created after the war by former prisoners, including contemporary works.

LIBRARY

The Library collection is appropriate to the nature of the museum. It includes books, periodicals and maps related to the Second World War, the Third Reich, the occupation, and martyrdom in the prisons and concentration camps, with special emphasis on Auschwitz concentration camp. The Library holds approximately 20,000 book volumes, over 2500 periodicals and 44 maps.

CONSERVATION DEPARTMENT

The Conservation Department deals with the protection and conservation of the grounds and buildings of the former Auschwitz concentration camp, as well as the post-war collections. The department collaborates with outstanding specialists and consultants from Poland and abroad. Some of the work is done by the museum preservation crew and some by specialized outside firms working under the supervision of and in collaboration with the Museum Preservation Officer. The department also carries out renovation, repairs and other work connected with the functioning of the museum, in co-operation with other museum organizational divisions.

HISTORICAL AND RESEARCH DEPARTMENT

The primary task of the Historical and Research Department is to carry out research on various aspects of the history of Auschwitz-

Birkenau concentration camp, and to make this work accessible in the form of scholarly books and articles, as well as publications intended for non-specialist readers.

Major accomplishments include collaboration with other researchers on the five-volume 1995 work entitled *Auschwitz 1940–1945: Central Issues in the History of the Camp*, whose authors are Danuta Czech, Tadeusz Iwaszko, Stanisław Kłodziński, Helena Kubica, Aleksander Lasik, Franciszek Piper, Irena Szczelecka, Andrzej Strzelecki and Henryk Świebocki. The editors are Wacław Długoborski and Franciszek Piper. Other works published by department staff include Danuta Czech's *Calendar of Events in Auschwitz Concentration Camp*, Franciszek Piper's *The Employment of Auschwitz Concentration Camp Prisoners* and *How Many People Died in Auschwitz Concentration Camp?*, Henryk Świebocki's *Reports by Escapees from Auschwitz Concentration Camp*, as well as numerous works in the series *Zeszyty Oświęcimskie (Auschwitz Journal)* and *Hefte von Auschwitz*.

Forthcoming titles include *The Destruction of the Polish Jews in Auschwitz Concentration Camp, The Destruction of Poles in Auschwitz Concentration Camp, The Fate of the Children from the Zamość Region, The Role of IG Farbenindustrie in the Exploitation of Slave Labor and the History of the Monowice Sub-Camp* and *The Fate of Women in Auschwitz Concentration Camp.*

DEPARTMENT FOR CONTACT WITH FORMER PRISONERS

This department collects all data about people deported to the camp. It plays a role in co-ordinating contacts with former prisoners on the part of various units of the museum organization. An important task is the completion of the card file based on a survey of former prisoners and their families by the department. Particular importance is attached to determining the names of people who were never entered in the camp records because they were killed in the gas chambers immediately after arrival. The department is compiling a file of names based on post-war publications, such as eyewitness accounts, memoirs, newspaper articles, films, and so on. The department is also co-ordinating work on the recording of interviews with former prisoners, as well as compiling name and subject indexes of materials in the museum collections.

EDUCATION DEPARTMENT

The Education Department disseminates information about Auschwitz concentration camp. Basic activities include co-operation with school students and teachers, Polish and foreign institutions, research institutions and youth study groups. Events organized by the department include lectures, readings, museum lessons, teachers' conferences, film symposia and screenings, drawing contests and concepts for the best papers on camp subjects. The department also collaborates in the organization of various public events including international meetings, rallies, marches and relays. Another important task is the provision of guide services for visitors through a specialized section, as well as documenting and analysing visitor traffic.

Since its founding, the museum has been visited by 25 million people from all over the world. Since 1990, there have been approximately 500,000 visitors per year, of whom approximately one-half are young people. Visitors from more than 100 foreign countries constitute 40–5 per cent of the visitors.

EXHIBITIONS DEPARTMENT

The most important tasks of the Exhibitions Department include the initiation, preparation, execution and organization of permanent and temporary exhibitions mounted on the grounds of the museum, as well as elsewhere in Poland and around the world. The 300 temporary and travelling exhibitions mounted during the 50-year history of the museum have been visited by approximately 15 million people. Exhibitions have been held in England, Czechoslovakia, Germany, Israel, Japan, the Netherlands, the USA, the former USSR, Sweden, Hungary, Italy, Switzerland and Austria. The department co-operates with various organizations and institutions in organizing exhibitions, as well as lending support to the organization of exhibitions by other institutions.

STATE MUSEUM PUBLISHERS

The publishers issue and distribute studies of subjects associated with the history of Auschwitz concentration camp and the activities of the museum, as well as co-operating with other publishers in Poland and abroad. To date, the publishers have brought out 420 titles in a total of 7 million copies. These include scientific studies, non-specialist studies, source publications, literature, poetry and memoirs, as well as albums, posters, postcards and video cassettes presenting the history of Auschwitz.

Should there be further questions concerning the educational aspects of the museum's mission, please contact us by phone at 033 8432022 or by fax at 033 8431934.

Chapter 7

Teaching the Holocaust in the United States

Samuel Totten

This chapter provides an overview of Holocaust education at the secondary (ages 12–18) and, to a lesser extent, the upper elementary levels (ages 10–12) in the United States. It comments on nationally recognized Holocaust education programmes, city and state sponsored Holocaust curricula, recommendations and mandates, the role of the United States Holocaust Memorial Museum in educating about this history, and some of the stronger instructional strategies and learning activities used by educators to teach this history.

The nature of Holocaust education in the United States is eclectic, largely due to the fact that United States public education is – as required by constitutional provision – decentralized. As a result, state departments of education, local school districts and individual teachers largely decide what is and is not to be taught in local schools. Thus, it is neither unusual nor surprising that individual educators, schools, school districts and states have taken the lead in Holocaust education.

Since no systematic study has been undertaken to assess how widespread Holocaust education is in the United States, it is impossible to state with certainty how many teachers, schools or school districts are involved in educating about the Holocaust, let alone to comment definitively on how they are teaching about this history. It is safe to say that due to certain Holocaust education programmes (e.g. Facing History and Ourselves), the establishment of two major Holocaust museums (the US Holocaust Memorial Museum in Washington, DC, and the Beit Hashoah Museum of Tolerance in Los Angeles), the support and assistance of Holocaust resource centres across the United States, and various state recommendations and mandates to teach about the Holocaust, that thousands of the hundreds of thousands of teachers in the United States are involved – to one extent or another – in teaching about the Holocaust.

Currently, the only way to ascertain how the Holocaust is taught in the United States is through an examination of articles, essays and dissertations written by teachers and masters and doctoral candidates; extant curricula developed and disseminated by Holocaust museums, resource centres, state departments of education, local school districts and individual teachers; reports issued by Holocaust museums and resource centres; papers and talks presented at pedagogical conferences, especially those whose sole focus is Holocaust education; one-on-one conversations with teachers; and visits to and observations of classrooms where the Holocaust is taught. Obviously, such an approach is highly unscientific.

When taught at all at the secondary level of schooling, the Holocaust is generally addressed in such courses as World History, US History or English. Much more rarely, an entire course on the Holocaust might be taught as an elective or one that is not required. A major problem, though, is that up to half of the students in elementary and secondary schools do not study world history or western civilization (Bradley Commission, cited in Sobol, 1988).

When taught at the upper elementary level (ages 10–12), what is generally used is an excerpt from the *Diary of Anne Frank*, a selection of poems from *I Never Saw Another Butterfly* and/or a short novel about a young person's travails during the Holocaust period.

NATIONALLY RECOGNIZED HOLOCAUST EDUCATION PROGRAMMES

One of the earliest and most influential educational programmes on the Holocaust is the Facing History and Ourselves (FHAO) programme. Founded in 1976 in Massachusetts by two junior high school teachers, the FHAO programme was developed to assist teachers to teach the universal themes of the history of the Holocaust through 'a rigorous examination of its particularities'. Purporting to use both content and methodology which promote critical thinking (such as one that purposely encourages cognitive dissonance by challenging students' simple answers to complex issues), reflection, and the need to make connections between the study of history and its relationship to one's own life and society, FHAO gradually expanded from a local to a regional to a nationwide programme.

Facing History reports that over 30,000 educators have been reached by the programme, and that those teachers have taught nearly 500,000 students about this history, using FHAO's philosophical approach and methodology.

Following a three-year period (1977–80) during which Facing History implemented, monitored and evaluated its teacher training and dissemination programme in various schools throughout New England, the US Department of Education's National Diffusion Network granted the programme its imprimatur which resulted in the Facing History programme being placed on the prestigious National Diffusion Network. As a result, Facing History was deemed an 'exemplary model programme worthy to be replicated across the nation'. Since the late 1970s the Facing History programme has been replicated in both secondary schools and universities throughout the USA and Canada. (To contact FHAO, write to: FHAO, 16 Hurd Road, Brookline, MA 02146, USA.)

Despite its resounding success as well as its wide acclaim by many (including members of the US Congress, noted historians and researchers, and educators at both secondary and university levels), FHAO has faced criticism. Speaking of FHAO's first curriculum volume (which was published in 1982), Dawidowicz (1992) asserted that the curriculum's focus was not solely the Holocaust, but rather 'a vehicle' for teaching students about civil disobedience and 'indoctrinating' them to favour nuclear disarmament. She also criticized Facing History for approaching the issue of antisemitism in a facile manner and couching antisemitism in the more general terms of scapegoating, prejudice and bigotry. In her most strident criticism, Dawidowicz claimed that Facing History overemphasized the importance of the issue of obedience to authority as being one of the key components of a totalitarian society while underplaying the fact that it is terror that is at the heart of such societies. Counter-arguments by proponents of Facing History claim that not all of Dawidowicz's criticism was fair. They claim that some of her points place her within the realm of the New Right who were and are critical of many current educational trends and practices including multi-cultural education and social responsibility educational initiatives, while other points place her in the camp with those Jewish opponents of Facing History who claim that the latter's approach undermines the uniqueness of the Holocaust (Fine, 1995).

Lipstadt (1995) has also criticized Facing History's curriculum, calling it 'deeply flawed'. Noting that Facing History is possibly the 'most influential model for teaching the Holocaust in the United States', her criticism is primarily aimed at the context in which the history of the Holocaust is placed. More specifically, she asserts that by attempting to inoculate students against prejudice by addressing such issues such as racism and violence in the USA, the curriculum 'elides the differences between the Holocaust and all manner of inhumanities and injustices' (Lipstadt, 1995, p. 27). Concomitantly, she asserts that by attempting to be relevant to a wide variety of parties, the curriculum, intentionally or not, encourages teachers to draw historically fallacious parallels which results in a distortion of history.

Another curricular programme, *A Holocaust Curriculum: Life Unworthy of Life: An 18-Lesson Instructional Unit* (Bolkosky, *et al.*, 1987) which was developed by the Center for the Study of the Child in Detroit, Michigan, is also part of the National Diffusion Network. Praised by many, including Dawidowicz (1992), it addresses the Holocaust through the 'stories of specific children, families' in order 'to uncover the human dimension of such inhumanity'. In Dawidowicz's (1992) opinion, due to its approach, accuracy and depth, it is one of the strongest curricula currently available. Many educators avoid implementing this programme due to its length, and that is because it would consume more time than they have to devote to this history.

CITY AND STATE SPONSORED HOLOCAUST CURRICULA, RECOMMENDATIONS AND MANDATES

Numerous school boards across the United States have endorsed and/or mandated the teaching of the Holocaust. Among these are Atlanta, Baltimore, Des Moines, Los Angeles, Milwaukee, New York City, Philadelphia and Pittsburgh. Scores of local school boards across the USA have also supported and/or required the study of the Holocaust in their schools. What this means in reality, though, is difficult to ascertain. In some cases, it may involve teaching a lesson for a single period of approximately 50 minutes or a unit (which could last five to ten class periods or more) on the Holocaust in a history or social studies course. In other cases, the Holocaust may be addressed through the study of a single volume such as the *Diary of Anne Frank* or Elie Wiesel's *Night*; in still other cases, it may mean that teachers are encouraged to address this history in their course when they deem it appropriate to do so. Such leeway may result in perfunctory coverage leaving the students bereft of real knowledge regarding the antecedents leading up to and resulting in the Holocaust, let alone the facts about the Nazis' annihilatory process to destroy the Jews and murder millions of others, such as Gypsies, Slavs, Soviet prisoners of war and political opponents.

As of 1998, five states (California, Florida, Illinois, New Jersey and New York) had mandated (required) the teaching of the Holocaust in their public schools. Ten other states (Connecticut, Georgia, Indiana, North Carolina, Ohio, Pennsylvania, South Carolina, Tennessee, Virginia and Washington) either recommend or encourage their public school personnel to teach about the Holocaust. Among the aforementioned states, some have developed state guidelines (California), a curriculum on the Holocaust and/or genocide (Connecticut, Florida, New Jersey, New York, Ohio, Pennsylvania, South Carolina and Virginia) and a study guide (Georgia).

The development of these curricula and teaching guides has also proved valuable in that typical social studies, government and literature textbooks generally have a dearth of information on the Holocaust. At best, the history of the Holocaust is allotted two to three pages, including pictures and sidebars (which often include excerpts from books, newspapers and first-person accounts). In light of the fact that the text often constitutes the curriculum in a vast majority of classes in public schools across the United States, resources such as curricular and teacher guides fill a serious vacuum.

It is one thing to require that a topic be taught, and an altogether different situation actually to teach it in an effective manner (accurately, comprehensively, thought-provokingly and meaningfully). Likewise, to 'encourage' or 'recommend' that something be taught is leaving the fate of any educational programme up to chance. If teachers are not interested in teaching about the Holocaust then there is certainly the possibility that they will not do so.

That said, the aforementioned city and state-sponsored programmes have 'legitimized' the Holocaust for many educators. They have provided teachers with important institutional support to teach about the Holocaust and in doing so, have paved the way for teachers to spend more classroom time on this history.

Dawidowicz (1992, p. 69) has noted that: 'most of the state-developed or sponsored Holocaust curricula are better at describing the events that took place during the Holocaust period than explaining why and how the Holocaust happened'. This is generally true of the vast majority of units and lessons developed by individual and/or teams of teachers. This results in a situation where students leave the study knowing some of the 'whats' but possibly none of the 'whys' of the Holocaust. Dawidowicz (1992) has correctly pointed out that this is particularly true of the long history of antisemitism as espoused in Christian doctrine and its influence upon the Nazis' racial policies (including how it constituted state policy versus simply individual behaviour) as well as the much neglected fact by educators that central to this débâcle was the fact that premeditated mass murder was an instrument of government and bureaucratic policy.

Furthermore, many of the city and state-developed or state-sponsored curricula and teacher guides as well as local community and teacher-developed curricular packages are bereft of clear rationales, sound pedagogical approaches (strong and well-developed objectives, age appropriate readings, thought-provoking activities) and the selection of accurate content that avoids oversimplification and/or incorrect information. Many curricula are also bereft of adequate depth on key topics. Furthermore, some curricula and teacher guides equate various human rights infractions and/or genocidal events with the Holocaust, thus universalizing the Holocaust and ignoring its uniqueness (Totten and Parsons, 1992).

Far too many curricula rely on questionable activities such as the use of simulations and role-playing exercises that purport to provide students with a sense as to what the victims experienced or the opportunity to assume how they would have acted under dire circumstances when faced with a tortuously complex moral dilemma. There is also a propensity to include simplistic learning activities such as crossword puzzles, 'find the term' in a block of letters, and other such gimmicks that are of dubious educational value (Totten and Parsons, 1992).

UNITED STATES HOLOCAUST MEMORIAL MUSEUM

As of September 1998, there were approximately fifty Holocaust resource centres, twelve memorials and nineteen Holocaust museums in the United States. The function of many of the centres and museums is to conduct public outreach programmes on various aspects of the Holocaust and/or support the teaching of the Holocaust in the local and regional school districts. Many centres assist schools in developing curricula, provide in-service programmes to teachers in private and public schools, and assist teachers and students in locating speakers (including survivors and liberators), films and adjunct materials. Many have also developed their own curricula.

The premier museum in the United States is the United States Holocaust Memorial Museum. The US Congressional mandate that formally established the museum mandated that the museum meet the needs of educators throughout the USA by providing them with key services (including staff development opportunities and pedagogical advice) and curricular and resource materials in order to facilitate teaching students about the Holocaust.

In addition to the educative nature of the museum's permanent exhibit (a three-floor exhibition that presents a comprehensive history of the Holocaust through artefacts, photographs, films and eye-witness testimonies), the museum accommodates scheduled school groups by providing an overview of the museum and the layout of its exhibit and, in certain cases, a debriefing session at the conclusion of the students' visit.

Another integral part of the museum's effort to meet the needs of teachers is the Resource Center which houses curricula and lesson plans developed by state departments of education, private organizations and individual teachers. Also included in the collection are bibliographies, filmographies and other adjunct teaching materials.

The museum has a learning centre where students and teachers, as well as members of the general public, can explore the Holocaust in more depth on one of the 24 touchscreen or multimedia workstations. In addition to studying information found in the *Encyclopedia of the Holocaust*, students and teachers can explore historical photographs, interviews with Holocaust survivors, documentary footage, historical audio recordings and maps.

As part of its educational outreach programme, the museum has developed a series of teaching materials. Among these materials are *Guidelines for Teaching about the Holocaust* (Parsons and Totten, 1994), an Artefact Poster Set (comprising coloured posters with photographs of artefacts on display in the permanent exhibit) and an accompanying teacher's guide, an annotated bibliography and an annotated filmography. All of the latter were specially prepared for use by educators at various levels of schooling (elementary through college). All of these resources (except the poster series) are free of charge, and available on the Internet (http://www.ushmm.org).

The museum also hosts and conducts numerous conferences (both on site as well as in various regions across the nation) on teaching about the Holocaust for teachers and administrators. One of its most innovative educational programmes is the Mandel Fellows Program, where teachers from across the United States are selected to undergo intensive training at the museum to become teacher consultants in their regions of the country. (To obtain additional information about the museum's educational programmes, write to: Director of Education, United States Holocaust Memorial Museum, 100 Raoul Wallenberg Place SW, Washington, DC 20024-2150.)

VARIOUS INSTRUCTIONAL STRATEGIES AND LEARNING ACTIVITIES USED IN TEACHING ABOUT THE HOLOCAUST

What is provided here is a broad overview of some of the most accurate, in-depth, soundly constructed teaching strategies and learning activities currently used by various educators across the United States to teach about various facets of Holocaust education. Prior to teaching the history, some teachers place a strong emphasis on pre-assessment activities, or ascertaining what the students know and do not know about the Holocaust (Totten, 1998). This may include having the students develop clusters or mind-maps (Rico, 1986, pp. 17–20) in which they delineate their understanding of all that is related to the target word 'Holocaust'. In this way teachers are able to assess the depth and sophistication of the students' knowledge as well as any inaccuracies or gaps in their knowledge-base and/or any myths they may hold. Other pre-assessment activities involve asking students why they wish to study this history or what they hope to learn, and/or any 'burning questions' they may have about the Holocaust that they want answered during the course of the study.

A component of many of the best units and lessons is the development of rationales for teaching this history. Often such rationales are developed and refined, as the unit progresses, by both the teacher and students. As the authors of the United States Holocaust Memorial Museum's *Guidelines for Teaching about the Holocaust* state:

> Because the objective of teaching any subject is to engage the intellectual curiosity of the student in order to inspire critical thought and personal growth, it is helpful to structure your lesson plan on the Holocaust by considering throughout questions of rationale. (Parsons and Totten, 1994, p. 1)

The strongest approaches to teaching this history involve the students in assessing and coming to understand not only what took place during the Holocaust period, but also why it took place. This involves ample study of those historical trends that 'combined to make the Holocaust possible' (Niewyk, 1995, p. 175) including but not limited to 'antisemitism, racism, social Darwinism, extreme nationalism, totalitarianism, industrialism, and the nature of modern war' (Niewyk, 1995, p. 175). Different teachers approach this effort in various ways.

Those teachers who desire their students to wrestle with this history, versus simply learn facts and recite them on an examination, may use, for example, a decision-making approach (Engle and Ochoa, 1988). In the decision-making approach the teacher's role is to stimulate thinking, encourage dialogue and guide students in evaluating the worth of ideas. The role of teachers becomes a facilitative one where teachers raise questions, foster doubt, present competing views, challenge the ideas of students and promote rigorous and democratic dialogue. At the same time, the teacher must be informed with respect to the issues under discussion (Engle and Ochoa, 1988, p. 162).

Still other teachers use a combination of the above approach along with a more didactic approach in which students are guided through a structured process in order to delineate and explore the historical antecedents, causes and ramifications of this history (Totten, 1998). More rigid than the decision-making approach, this process ensures that students become conversant with the historical trends that ultimately culminated in the Holocaust as well as the key periods, events, people and chronology of the history. This approach does not and should not preclude students from grappling with the import, consequences and moral ramifications of this history in order to construct understanding (Wieser, 1995; Totten, 1998).

Part and parcel of the above approaches is the interpretation of primary source documents (Kalfus, 1990). Among the most effective methods used in such an approach is to provide the students with the 'tools' for interpreting historical evidence, including a solid foundation in the history of the period as well as requisite analytical skills. The latter includes the following: the critical need to identify the author/source of the document, the date of the document, the recipient of the document and the type of document (letter, memorandum, and so on); delineate the stated purpose of the document; note word choice, including euphemisms and possible code words; note the tone of the document (matter of fact, ironic, sarcastic, derogatory, pleading); identify any underlying meaning; recognizing essential information versus non-essential information; recognition of key allusions, including those to key historical events of the period.

Some curricula and teachers use case studies to deepen their students' thinking about key concepts and/or situations germane to the Holocaust. For example, a typical activity involves students studying 'actual case studies of German citizens ... designed to give the history meaning in terms of an average German citizen as decision-maker' (Strom and Parsons, 1982, p. 88). The directions for the activity are:

divide the class into seven groups and assign a case study to each group. Ask each group to review the ten points of the Nazi plan and the two party platforms and then determine which of the parties the person in each case study would choose. Be sure each groups has reason to support its choice. (Strom and Parsons, 1982, p. 88)

Many teachers in the fields of social studies and English use literature (novels, novellas, short stories, poetry and memoirs) to illuminate various aspects of the history (Totten, 1996). One of the most powerful ways of doing so is through the use of reader response theory (Purves *et al.*, 1995). Basically,

in reader-response theory, the text's meaning is considered to reside in the 'transaction' between the reader and the text, not from the text alone ... In practice, reader-response theory considers very carefully how students respond intellectually and emotionally to the text ... By validating students' responses, teachers can spark a lively discussion from which a careful literary analysis will flow. (O'Neill, 1994, p. 7).

A powerful way to accomplish the latter is to place Dan Pagis' (1989) poem 'Written in Pencil in a Sealed Boxcar' on an overhead transparency and simply ask the students to write a letter to the poet in regard to their gut response to the poem. The response may address anything the students wish, including their curiosity about aspects of the poem, their appreciation or dislike of the poem, a guess at what it means, and so on. Once the letters are completed, students are placed in small groups to discuss their responses. As they engage in discussion they are directed to use one another's responses in order to probe ever-deeper into the possible meaning of the poem. Finally, a large class discussion is held to share the responses of the various groups and to continue to probe the reactions and insights to the poem (see Totten, forthcoming).

Both Holocaust curricula and individual teachers incorporate first-person accounts of survivors, liberators and others to help illustrate key aspects of the Holocaust (Totten, 1994). Among the purposes for doing so are to delineate the complexity of choices made by and/or foisted on people during the Holocaust period, to personalize the study by adding specific and personal detail to the history, and to illuminate various periods and aspects of the Holocaust years. Teachers use various activities to engage their students in the use of first-person accounts. For example, some require students to keep journals throughout the study for the purpose of illuminating key themes, time periods, events or individuals. Teachers may also use first-person accounts to assist students to compare and contrast the type of information found in historical essays, primary documents and/or fictional works. Some teachers have their students watch and analyse videotape accounts of survivors (Facing History and Ourselves, 1989). Finally, many invite survivors and liberators to class to speak to the students, and/or have students conduct interviews with survivors and/or liberators.

CONCLUSION

With the opening of the United States Holocaust Memorial Museum in April 1993, there has been a renewed and powerful wave of interest among educators in the United States to teach about the Holocaust. More and more educational journals are including articles and essays on teaching about the Holocaust; as a result, an ever-increasing number of teachers are beginning to share their ideas, methods and successes. There are several Internet listserves (including H-NET List for History of the Holocaust < H-HOLOCAUST@H-NET.MSU.EDU >) whose focus is teaching about the Holocaust; these, too, provide an avenue for educators in the public schools, colleges and universities to discuss both historical and pedagogical issues germane to teaching about the Holocaust as well as to share information about resources. As a result of such efforts, the field of Holocaust studies is slowly but surely becoming more sophisticated and pedagogically sound.

Still, there is a dire need for educational researchers to begin to study every facet of Holocaust education in order to ascertain the efficacy of such pedagogical endeavours. Until that is done, educators and others are likely to develop resources and teach about the Holocaust in a manner that is based more on intuition and trial and error than what is proved to be most efficacious in assisting students to learn and grapple with this complex history.

REFERENCES

Bolkosky, S.M., Ellisa, B.R. and Harris, D. (1987) *A Holocaust Curriculum: Life Unworthy of Life: An 18-Lesson Instructional Unit*. Farmington Hills, MI: Center for the Study of the Child.
Dawidowicz, L. (1992) How they teach the Holocaust. In Dawidowicz, *What is the Use of Jewish History?* New York: Schocken Books.
Engle, S. and Ochoa, A. (1988) *Education for Democratic Citizenship: Decision-Making in the Social Studies*. New York: Teachers College Press.
Facing History and Ourselves (1989) *Facing History and Ourselves: Elements of Time – Holocaust Testimonies*. Brookline, MA: FHAO.
Fine, M. (1995) *Habits of Mind: Struggling Over Values in America's Classrooms*. San Francisco, CA: Jossey-Bass.

Kalfus, R. (1990) Euphemisms of death: interpreting a primary source document on the Holocaust, *The History Teacher*, **23**(2), 87–93.

Lipstadt, D. (1995) Not facing history, *The New Republic,* 6 March, 27, 29.

Niewyk, D.L. (1995) Holocaust: the genocide of the Jews. In S. Totten, W.S. Parsons, and I.W. Charny, (eds) *Genocide in the Twentieth Century: Critical Essays and Eyewitness Accounts*. New York: Garland.

O'Neill, J. (1994) Rewriting the book on literature: changes sought in how literature is taught – what students read, *ASCD Curriculum Update*, **June**, 7, 8.

Pagis, D. (1989) *Variable Directions: The Selected Poetry of Dan Pagis*. San Francisco, CA: North Point Press.

Parsons, W.S. and Totten, S. (1994) *Guidelines for Teaching about the Holocaust*. Washington, DC: United States Holocaust Memorial Museum.

Purves, A.C., Rogers, T., and Soter, A.O. (1995) *How Porcupines Make Love III: Readers, Texts, Cultures in the Response-Based Literature Classroom*. White Plains, NY: Longman.

Rico, G.L. (1986) Clustering: a prewriting process. In C. Booth Olson (ed.) *Practical Ideas for Teaching Writing as Process*. Sacramento, CA: California State Department of Education.

Sobol, M. (1995) Holocaust education in the United States. Unpublished paper.

Strom, M.S. and Parsons, W.S. (1982*) Facing History and Ourselves: Holocaust and Human Behavior*. Watertown, MA: Intentional Educations.

Totten, S. (1994) The use of first-person accounts in teaching about the Holocaust, *British Journal of Holocaust Education*, **3**(2), 160–83.

Totten, S. (1996) Using literature to teach about the Holocaust, *Journal of Holocaust Education*, **5**(1), 14–48.

Totten, S. (1998) The start is as important as the finish: establishing a foundation for the study of the Holocaust, *Social Education*, **62**(2), 70–6.

Totten, S. (ed.) (forthcoming) *Teaching Holocaust Literature*. Needham Heights, MA: Allyn and Bacon.

Totten, S. and Parsons, W.S. (1992) State developed teacher guides and curricula on genocide and/or the Holocaust: a review and critique, *Inquiry in Social Studies: Curriculum, Research, and Instruction: The Journal of the North Carolina Council for Social Studies*, **28**(1), 27–47.

Wieser, P. (1995) Anti-Semitism: a warrant for genocide, *Social Education* (special issue, Teaching about the Holocaust), **59**(6), C4–C6.

Chapter 8

Teaching the Holocaust in England

Susan Hector

This chapter is concerned with the present state of Holocaust teaching in secondary schools in England. The impact of the Education Reform Act 1988 on Holocaust teaching is explored and research findings over recent years are discussed. Recommendations regarding best practice in England conclude the chapter.

THE HOLOCAUST IN THE CURRICULUM

Fox's (1989) study into the extent to which the Holocaust was being taught in British schools looked only at what was happening in history lessons. He discovered a dismal picture and suggested that 'probably more attention was being paid to the subject of the Holocaust in departments other than those of history'. This was absolutely right. Had he looked more closely, he would have noticed that the Holocaust was being taught in a number of departments. In English, for example, the Holocaust was (and is still) to be found within studies on the media or propaganda for older students while for younger ones, Anne Frank's diary is still a favoured text. Other Holocaust-related literature is also to be discovered in English lessons including *When Hitler Stole Pink Rabbit* (Kerr, 1971), *Friedrich* (Richter, 1970) and more recently, *But Can the Phoenix Sing?* (Laird, 1993) and *Tell No One Who You Are* (Buchignani, 1994).

Lessons on the Holocaust are also a feature of personal, social and moral education curricula where a popular approach is through discussions on bullying, prejudice and racism. The Holocaust is often evident too in specially designed general studies classes for older students and in A level German lessons the Holocaust is sometimes explored within, for example, a study of the *Literatur der Nazizeit* (Literature of the Nazi Period). While it might seem appropriate to teach about the Holocaust within geography, this is not the case to date in the secondary sector, although a study of the Holocaust is sometimes found within programmes on tourism in colleges of further education.

Fox completely overlooked one major contributor to Holocaust teaching, namely religious education. Had he spotted this, he would have discovered that the Holocaust featured in the programmes of study in several agreed syllabuses for RE as well as in religious studies public examination courses. Additionally, the Holocaust was (and is) taught through art, often in collaboration with coursework requirements for other public examination subjects, for example GCSE religious studies, and frequently as part of an assessment exercise at the end of a history or RE programme of study for younger students.

The British government's push towards a compulsory Education for Citizenship strategy in schools in the wake of the recommendations of the Stephen Lawrence Report may prove yet another vehicle for Holocaust studies in England. It will be interesting to see how this develops.

HOLOCAUST TEACHING AND THE NATIONAL CURRICULUM

Until 1988 it is fair to say that teaching about the Holocaust in England was rather a hit-and-miss affair, dependent upon individual teachers' interests. Then its importance was recognized at national level. The Education Reform Act, the most significant piece of education legislation in England and Wales for more than forty years, was passed. The National Curriculum which emerged provided schools with strict guidelines regarding subject content at each of the Key Stages throughout a child's school career. Teachers, academics and others anxious to see a place for Holocaust teaching in the Orders for History lobbied the government hard over the next two years. When the final report was published in 1990, not only was the 'Era of the Second World War: 1933–1948' included in the core, that is, the compulsory section of the Orders but the Holocaust was specifically mentioned as a component for study and assessment purposes. In spite of opposition from some quarters, notably from Kochan (1989), this seemed to guarantee that all children in the state school system in England and Wales would learn about the Holocaust at age 14.

TEACHING THE HOLOCAUST THROUGH HISTORY

Though the Holocaust may be taught across a range of subjects, history appears to be the 'natural' place for the study of the Holocaust, especially when the focus of Key Stage 3 teaching is 'The Twentieth Century World', where a range of GCSE history syllabuses examine Nazi Germany – for example, Midland Examining Group (MEG) 1607, Edexcel 3325B, Southern Examining Group (SEG) 2720, Northern and East Anglian Board (NEAB) 1328 – and where the subject remains a popular choice for in-depth A level studies, for example, Associated Examining Board (AEB) 673, Edexcel 9267, NEAB 42.

My survey (Hector 1999) into history teachers' attitudes to teaching the Holocaust revealed varying degrees of commitment. While several offered purely pragmatic reasons for teaching it ('It's on the syllabus'), most history teachers questioned concurred with this response: 'As History becomes optional after Year 9, no pupil ought to end their academic study of the subject without looking at the depths to which mankind can descend.'

Most teachers lamented the lack of time available, in their view, to do the subject justice. Many just managed to teach it across two to five lessons. One commented, 'We have only 26 lessons to teach the whole Twentieth Century World Module (at Key Stage 3), therefore 3 lessons is all we can allow even though we know that isn't really long enough.'

As a text, teachers have found Supple's (1993) comprehensive *From Prejudice to Genocide* a useful starting point for themselves and their students while Landau's (1992) *The Nazi Holocaust* and Burleigh and Wippermann's (1991) *The Racial State: Germany 1933–1945* are good basic texts for teachers and older students wanting to get to grips with the subject. Bresheeth *et al.*'s (1994) *The Holocaust for Beginners* is another useful starter text for students.

The publication of Carrie Supple's key text was a response to what she saw as a dearth of good Holocaust materials available to teachers in 1989 when she carried out her research (Supple, 1992). She urged teachers to enable their pupils to empathize with the victims, to see them as real people with names and histories. 'Children can't grasp the idea of six million nameless victims: to present the period in that way is to risk paralysing and incapacitating them. It must be made touchable' (Klein, 1992). One way of achieving this, teachers have found, is to focus on the lives of key people in the Holocaust and one method of doing this is through the use of video in the classroom.

Spielberg's *Schindler's List* is the most frequently found Holocaust video in English schools, not least because of Spielberg's generosity in donating a specially edited version to every secondary school in the UK. Jack Gold's *Escape from Sobibor* (CBS-TV, 1987) is another common choice. In spite of its age and its approach, many history teachers continue to show extracts from *The World at War: Genocide* (Thames TV, 1972) while others use the much more recent *The Nazis: A Warning from History* (BBC TV, 1997). In my survey (Hector, 1999) there was, surprisingly, no mention made of *People's Century: 1933 Master Race* (BBC TV, 1995), possibly the most succinct survey on video of what the Holocaust was all about and conspicuously suitable for classroom use.

Teachers in England are fortunate enough to be able to take advantage of a wide range of other resources available from, for example, the Anne Frank Educational Trust (4th Floor, 43 Portland Place, London W1N 3AG, tel. 020 8340 9077). School visits to its travelling exhibition can be arranged and groups of schools can request that the Trust sets up its exhibition for those schools for a limited period. A comprehensive resource pack, *Lessons of the Holocaust*, has been produced by the Spiro Institute for the Study of Jewish History and Culture (The Old House, c/o King's College London, Kidderpore Avenue, London, NW3 7SZ , tel. 0207 431 0345) in collaboration with the Holocaust Educational Trust (BCM Box 7892, London WC1N 3XX, tel. 020 7222 6822/5853) from which a number of other resources and services can be obtained, including arranging for Holocaust survivors to speak to school groups.

The *Bergen-Belsen Exhibition* at the Imperial War Museum (Lambeth Road, London, SE1 6HZ, tel. 020 7416 5000) offers special arrangements to teachers wishing to take groups of schoolchildren over the age of 14. Beth Shalom Holocaust Memorial Centre (Laxton, Newark, Notts. NG22 0PA, tel. 01623 836627) welcomes school parties to its permanent exhibition, offers to set up exhibitions in individual schools and is able to provide guest speakers.

An increasing number of schools now undertake educational visits to Prague and Theresienstadt (Terezin) (Hector, 1994) or to Krakow and Auschwitz, given the relatively cheap costs and ease of access to these locations since the collapse of the Eastern Bloc. Additionally, students studying German at GCSE or A level may well visit Dachau or Sachsenhausen camps on cultural exchanges to Munich or Berlin.

Not least, several history texts have been specially written to respond to the National Curriculum's inclusion of the Holocaust at Key Stage 3. These include Kelly and Whittock (1993), Brooman (1993) and DeMarco and Radway (1995). While not necessarily devoting more than one page to the subject, these authors nevertheless include the Holocaust as a major factor in the story of the twentieth century. Other more focused texts for student use include Grey and Little (1997) and Whittock (1995). Additionally, A level students and their teachers are able to have access to the extensive collection of Holocaust-related books from the Institute of Contemporary History and Wiener Library (4 Devonshire Street, London, W1N 2BH, tel. 020 7636 7247).

TEACHING THE HOLOCAUST THROUGH RELIGIOUS EDUCATION

Although history might seem the 'natural' location for Holocaust education to take place and notwithstanding its inclusion by other subjects, the Holocaust sits particularly comfortably within religious education. Quite independently of the Holocaust's inclusion in history programmes of study, teachers of religious education have been involved in teaching the subject for a number of years whether as part of a GCSE or A level religious studies syllabus or within agreed syllabus guidelines. (As we shall see later, through a programme which begins in the primary school to one which ends when pupils complete their secondary education, children in England and Wales follow courses in religious education which enable them to become familiar with key concepts, beliefs, values, practices, history and customs of up to six major world religions, including Christianity.)

Perhaps because RE teachers feel a little more confident than do others in teaching about a subject that has so much to do with death, they frequently opt to teach the Holocaust wherever they find the opportunity to do so. Whereas in history we might say the focus in Holocaust teaching is on learning *about* the subject, in RE a slightly different picture emerges: the focus is on learning *from* the Holocaust. Additionally, in the words of Stradling *et al.* (1984), teachers of religious education tend to adopt either the 'product-based' approach where what is important is the subject matter itself (where the Holocaust is studied, for example, within a broad-sweep look at Judaism in Years 7 or 8 for 12–14 year olds) or the 'process-based' approach where the subject matter is of less importance than the skills the young person uses and develops (where the Holocaust is used as a case study, for example, in work in Years 9 or 10 on 'Prejudice and Human Rights' or 'Peace and Conflict'). The Holocaust is a specific area to be studied within GCSE religious studies syllabuses (both traditional and short course,) including MEG 1730 and NEAB 1342 and at A level, for example, Edexcel 9560, OCR (Oxford Cambridge and RSA Examinations).

A major challenge immediately presents itself to RE teachers. Clearly, if the agreed syllabus requires it, one of their major roles is to teach about Judaism. Short's (1991a) survey into children's attitudes to Jews and Judaism highlighted the need for Judaism to be taught accurately and sympathetically if later Holocaust studies are to be effective. Later he warned that 'learning about Judaism will not necessarily diminish antisemitism. Indeed, if taught badly, it could exacerbate it' (Short 1991b). Teachers of religious education have taken heed of Short's warning and are rising to the challenge.

So that teachers do not unwittingly reinforce the negative victim stereotype (which Kochan (1989) also warned against), one of Short's main recommendations following his 1994–5 study was that teachers should explore with their students the roles played by other groups involved in the Holocaust, especially other victims (Short, 1995). Short's suggestion was welcomed by religious education teachers. In RE current students will not only investigate the story of Anne Frank, for example, but also explore what happened to the Gypsies or Jehovah's Witnesses, look at the role played by, say, Raoul Wallenberg in saving Hungarian Jews, consider the arguments given by key perpetrators for persecuting their victims and think about the parts played by the bystanders near at hand and perhaps even those further afield, the Allies. Having learned *about* these key players, students will be encouraged to consider their own positions, perhaps in relation to their current guarded treatment of a newcomer to the class or their attitude to a local influx of refugees from a war zone, and thus learn *from* their Holocaust lessons.

In the current educational climate, teachers in English schools are used to recommending and sharing resources, particularly in terms of textbooks suitable for classroom use. In addition to those produced for history and personal, social and moral education, several specifically RE textbooks contain Holocaust-related material, for example, Forta (1989), Jenkins (1992) and Lovelace and White (1996). More often than not, though, teachers produce their own study guides for their students, both at Key Stage 3 and examination level. Many more use their own resources for teaching the subject such as posters, postcards and slides brought back from private visits to Auschwitz and Yad Vashem. Some schools organize visits to Israel for their students as part of their RE studies and such visits often include a day spent at Yad Vashem.

As in history, videos play a central role in RE lessons. Popular choices include *Dear Kitty* (Anne Frank Centre, 1987) and *The Hiding Place* (1977) which tells the story of Christian Corrie ten Boom who risks her life in occupied Haarlem to hide Jews from the Nazis. Spielberg's *Schindler's List* is also used frequently in RE lessons. Not surprisingly, the focus is frequently upon the Holocaust's religious aspects. 'Where was God?' is a typical examination question. Teachers explore such questions with their students by examining the responses made by Elie Wiesel, Primo Levi and Hugo Gryn, for example.

In addition to the available resources mentioned earlier, RE teachers may seek out the services of the Jewish Education Bureau (8 Westcombe Avenue, Leeds, LS8 2BS, tel. 0113 266 3613) which is able to advise on and supply books, posters, artefacts, videos and speakers. Teachers may also contact the Education Department at Yad Vashem (PO Box 3477, Jerusalem 91034, Israel) for posters, slide sets, and audio- and video-resources and the Resource Centre for Educators, US Holocaust Memorial Museum (100 Raoul Wallenberg Place SW, Washington, DC 20024-2150, education@ushmm.org) for a teachers' catalogue which details all the books, posters and videos it has available. The specialist academic *Journal of Holocaust Education* is published twice a year. (It is available on subscription from Frank Cass & Co. Ltd, 900 Eastern Avenue, Newbury Park, Ilford, Essex IG2 7HH, tel. 020 8599 8866.)

Many teachers and their students are using CD-ROM and the Internet for yet more information, finding *The Teachers' Guide to the Holocaust* on the Web quite helpful, but it should be noted that the Internet also contains much scurrilous Holocaust denial material.

A CASE STUDY OF GOOD PRACTICE IN HOLOCAUST TEACHING

Wood Green School is a mixed comprehensive of 1100 pupils situated in a small market town west of Oxford. Pupils come from a wide catchment area and from a range of family backgrounds. The religious education department, in conjunction with the history department, organizes an annual Holocaust Study Day for Year 9 pupils. The Holocaust is studied in the classroom over eighteen lessons and the Study Day is its culmination. The head of department had sought help from the Spiro Institute in choosing and locating two Holocaust survivors.

The day begins with Year 9 gathered together, with their teachers, in order to set the mood, one of quiet contemplation. The head of department briefly explains the order of the day to the pupils before introducing the two visitors. Then candles are lit and the short act of remembrance begins, as one member of staff reads an extract from Anne Frank's diary and another shows appropriate slides. This is followed by other readings from Martin Niemoeller's poem and extracts from Elie Wiesel's *Night*. After a few quiet moments of reflection, the head of department explains that the year group will be divided into two, with the first remaining behind to listen to the first visitor while the second group goes elsewhere to listen to the second. After an hour, during which time the survivors each tell their stories to their groups, the young people are able to ask questions. After a break, the pupils watch the film *The Hiding Place*. Pupils have the afternoon to create their own personal response to the morning's events, either in the form of a poem or through a piece of artwork such as a poster or a model. Teachers are on hand during the afternoon's session for guidance.

Thus, over the course of several weeks, the students not only learn *about* the Holocaust in terms of knowledge and understanding of the historical events but also learn *from* the Holocaust, beginning to make connections between the survivors' experiences and their own lives.

CONCLUSION

Six significant factors which contribute to good Holocaust education emerge from the recent survey (Hector, 1999) referred to in this chapter of how the Holocaust is taught in England. The most significant factor is that close collaboration between subjects in which the Holocaust is taught is perceived to be desirable by teachers. It seems that where this happens, three things occur. First of all, the time allocation given to the subject increases significantly. Second, the opportunities for young people both to learn about and learn from the Holocaust can be identified by each subject and then focused on sharply, confident that both aspects are being properly considered overall. Third, young people appreciate the implicit message that Holocaust education is important enough to be taught in several major subject areas.

The second significant factor concerns pupils' education before they approach the Holocaust. As Short (1991b stresses, for good Holocaust education there needs to be good religious education. Poor RE can be counter-productive. Where good RE takes place, pupils will be at least beginning to grasp the need to 'develop a positive attitude towards other people, respecting their right to hold beliefs different from their own, and towards living in a society of diverse religions' (School Curriculum and Assessment Authority (SCAA), 1994). This will go some way to answering Short's concerns about reinforcing prejudices.

A third significant factor in ensuring effective Holocaust education is where, in religious education, pupils have already undergone a thorough grounding in what it means to be a Jew at the present time. This means that teachers must make clear to pupils that Jews may be religious or may have no faith at all. Only in this way will young people begin to appreciate Jews as ordinary human beings living ordinary lives and be able to make the connection that these ordinary people were Hitler's targets. More important still is the message to young people that the Jews' story is one of survival and creativity, not suffering.

The fourth significant factor in good Holocaust education is where the Holocaust is taught for its own sake, rather than being taught as a case study. Young people will quickly pick up the implicit message that the Holocaust is only one example among many that the teacher could have chosen and thus not really important. Harris (1989) has demonstrated very clearly what happens when something as significant as the Holocaust is left out of the curriculum. It is somehow even more problematic when the subject is treated in a half-hearted way. If teachers ensure that young people 'learn from' as well as 'learn about' the Holocaust, they will *per se* understand its lessons about prejudice and racism.

A fifth factor in effective Holocaust education concerns the amount of time given to the subject. Schools in England vary hugely in their allocation of time, some giving the Holocaust just a cursory mention in the course of one lesson while others devote a term's, half-term's or whole day to its study. Short (1995, p. 38) noted that 'it is debatable whether covering the Holocaust superficially is preferable to not covering it at all'.

The sixth contributory factor to good Holocaust education has to do with resources. Holocaust education is likely to be more effective where a variety of both primary and secondary source materials is used across a range of media and where care has been taken in their choice. Above all, Holocaust education works where young people have the chance to meet and interact with a Holocaust survivor in their own classroom. Nick (age 13) commented, 'It's different reading it in a book to actually hearing it from someone who actually experienced it'. Joanna (age 13) thought that one of the advantages of having a survivor speak to her class was that 'they can answer questions' and for Josie (age 13) its importance lay in the fact that she could see for herself that 'not everyone died'. In personal terms, too, these young people understood the importance of what they had learned. Richard (age 14) wondered how he would have coped in the situation described by the visitor. Amy (age 13) considered how she could have helped Jews, had she been born 60 years earlier, and explored the question of luck and chance in human existence.

REFERENCES

Bresheeth, H., Hood, S. and Jansz, L. (1994) *The Holocaust for Beginners*. Cambridge: Icon.

Brooman, J. (1993) *The Era of the Second World War*. London: Longman.

Buchignani, W. (1994) *Tell No One Who You Are*. London: Puffin.

Burleigh, M. and Wippermann, W. (1991) *The Racial State: Germany 1933–1945*. Cambridge: Cambridge University Press.

DeMarco, N. and Radway, R. (1995) *The Twentieth Century World*. Cheltenham: Stanley Thornes.

Forta, A. (1989) *Examining Religions: Judaism*. London: Heinemann.

Fox, J.P. (1989) *Teaching the Holocaust: The Report of a Survey in the United Kingdom*. Leicester: National Yad Vashem Charitable Trust and Centre for Holocaust Studies, University of Leicester.

Grey, P. and Little, R. (1997) *Germany 1918–1945*. Cambridge: Cambridge University Press.

Harris, M. (1989) Teaching the Null Curriculum: the Holocaust, *British Journal of Religious Education*, 11(3), summer, 136–8.

Hector, S.J. (1994) Prague Spring, *R.E. Today*, 11(3), summer, 36–7.

Hector, S.J. (1999) Teaching the Holocaust in secondary schools in south-central England. Unpublished MS, School of Education, Westminster College, Oxford.

Jenkins, J. (1992) *Contemporary Moral Issues*. Oxford: Heinemann Educational.

Kelly, N. and Whittock, M. (1993) *The Era of the Second World War*. London: Heinemann.

Kerr, J. (1971) *When Hitler Stole Pink Rabbit*. London: HarperCollins.

Klein, R. (1992) Facing up to the final solution, *The Times Educational Supplement*, 17 April, pp. 31–2.

Kochan, L. (1989) Life over death, *Jewish Chronicle*, 22 December, 25.

Laird, C. (1993) *But Can the Phoenix Sing?* London: Julia MacRae.

Landau, R. (1992) *The Nazi Holocaust*. London: Tauris.

Lovelace, A. and White, J. (1996) *Beliefs, Values and Traditions*. London: Heinemann.

Richter, H-P. (1970) *Friedrich*. London: Puffin.

School Curriculum and Assessment Authority (SCAA, now Qualifications and Curriculum Authority) (1994) *Model Syllabuses for Religious Education*. London: SCAA.

Short, G. (1991a) Teaching the Holocaust: some reflections on a problematic area, *British Journal of Religious Education*, **14**(1), autumn, 28–34.

Short, G. (1991b) Combating antisemitism: a dilemma for anti-racist education, *British Journal of Educational Studies*, **39**(1), 33–44.

Short, G. (1995) The Holocaust in the National Curriculum: a survey of teachers' attitudes and practices, *Journal of Holocaust Education*, **4**, 167–88.

Stradling, R., Noctor, M. and Baines, B. (1984) *Teaching Controversial Issues*. London: Edward Arnold.

Supple, C. (1992) The teaching of the Nazi Holocaust in North Tyneside, Newcastle and Northumberland secondary schools. Unpublished MS, School of Education, Newcastle upon Tyne.

Supple, C. (1993) *From Prejudice to Genocide: Learning about the Holocaust*. Stoke-on-Trent: Trentham Books.

Whittock, M. (1995) *Hitler and National Socialism*. London: Heinemann.

Part 3

Case Studies of Teaching and Learning about the Holocaust

Chapter 9

Teaching the Holocaust through English

Nicholas McGuinn

The educationalist Edward Blishen was a schoolboy during the period when Hitler was coming to power. Looking back on his school days, Blishen describes the teacher of English who made the greatest impact on him – a Welshman by the name of Williams. There was nothing of the Aryan 'superman' about this schoolmaster. Williams was small, with a high-pitched, sing-song voice. His students had no problem in sidetracking him from the work in hand. He was never known to finish a set book with his examination classes. But, for all that, Blishen still regarded Williams as a charismatic teacher because, crucially, he had 'a feeling for words and for what they could do' (Blishen, 1978, p. 133). This is the fundamental concern of English teachers. It is what marks them out from their colleagues; because of this, it is on the terrain of language that they must engage with the Holocaust.

THE NAZIS' MANIPULATION OF LANGUAGE

The Nazis mounted a fundamental assault upon the integrity of words. They understood only too well the importance of advice given by the Greek philosopher Plato to would-be educationalists over two thousand years ago: 'our first business is to supervise the production of stories, and choose only those we think suitable, and reject the rest' (Lee, 1987, p. 72).

One of Hitler's most powerful opening strategies was to 'supervise the production of stories' in the broadest sense of the phrase – by depriving Jewish people of the means of communicating with each other and with the outside world. The Nazis organized public burnings of books by Jewish authors, expelled Jews from German schools and universities, and replaced Jewish street names. Jews were forbidden to possess radios or phones. They were isolated within ghettos where they were denied access to other Jews, the German people as a whole and the wider global community. Carrie Supple quotes a schoolchild's chilling saying of the period: 'Dear God, strike me dumb, so that I shan't be sent to Dachau' (Supple, 1992, p. 78).

The Nazis themselves had the strongest 'feeling for words and for what they could do'. Just as they sought to deny Jewish people access to the channels of communication, so they manipulated the spoken and written word to their own ends. As a child, Hitler would 'practise "long and fervent sermons" standing on a kitchen table' (Supple, 1992, p. 61). He proved himself to be adept in the arts of rhetoric, mesmerizing audiences with his powers of oratory. The Nazis were experts in the creation and dissemination of mass propaganda. Julius Streicher published a popular newspaper, *The Stormer*, which sold over half a million copies weekly. Here, and in such works for children as *The Poisonous Mushroom* by Ernst Heimer (1938), he was able to foment hatred against the Jews on a national scale. Magazines such as *Mother and Folk* helped to construct the Aryan ideal of womanhood. If radios were denied to the Jews, they were provided cheaply to the rest of the German people, so that Nazi propaganda could be delivered straight to the workplace or the home. No form of the written or spoken word was regarded as too humble to serve the Nazi cause. The more populist the medium, in fact, the better. The Nazis made use, not only of cinema and advertising, but also of graffiti and racist slogans daubed on shop windows.

Postmodern critical theory has highlighted for us the essential instability of all sign systems; the Nazis, however, did particular violence to the relationship between signifier and signified. The notorious slogan attributed to Hitler's Minister of Propaganda, Joseph Goebbels, says it all: 'If you tell a lie, tell a big lie. If you tell it often enough, people will eventually believe you' (Supple, 1992, p. 69).

The Nazis lied on a massive scale. One of their most important words – 'Aryan' – is misused so that it bears a racist rather than linguistic meaning, and it is almost incredible to read with hindsight the 25-point programme of the National Socialist German Workers' Party issued in 1920. Here are just three examples from that document:

20. We demand the education at the public expense of specially gifted children of poor parents, without regard to the latter's position or occupation.
23. We demand laws to fight against *deliberate* political lies and their dissemination by the press.
24. We demand freedom for all religious denominations, provided they do not endanger the existence of the State or offend the concepts of decency and morality of the German race. (Landau, 1998, pp. 58–9)

Whether inveigling Jews on to concentration camp transports with promises of 'resettlement in the East' or admonishing gas chamber victims to be sure to leave their clothes in neat piles so they might find them more easily when they returned from their 'showers', the Nazis lied to deadly effect.

The Nazis engaged, too, in a grotesque use of euphemism (Marrus, 1988). Thus the phrase 'Night and Fog' refers not to a description of the weather and the time of day but to a decree passed in December 1939 which gave the secret police free rein to do what they liked with political dissidents. 'Crystal Night' is not the title of a piece of music or a painting but the name given to an act of organized violence which took place in November 1938 when the Nazis turned on the Jewish community, arresting 31,000, murdering 98 and destroying synagogues, shops and homes. 'Heaven Road' is not Berlin's equivalent of the Champs-Elysées in Paris but the phrase used by the guards at Treblinka concentration camp to describe the approach to the gas chambers.

The Nazis used language to dehumanize their victims and to distance themselves from their own criminality. Concentration camp inmates were tattooed and colour coded. Hitler described the 'Jewish race' as 'a parasite living on the body and the productive work of other nations'. To Heinrich Himmler, head of the SS, they were 'a bacillus' (Landau, 1998, pp. 67, 79). Particularly chilling is this government memorandum of 5 June 1942:

Since December 1941, ninety-seven thousand have been processed by the three vehicles in service, with no major incidents. In the light of observations made so far, however, the following technical changes are needed. (Landau, 1998, p. 35)

The 'vehicles' are mobile gas chambers. The 'processed' 97,000 are murdered human beings. The memorandum is entitled 'Secret Reich Business'.

The Russian critic and linguistic theorist, Mikhail Bakhtin – himself no stranger to totalitarian oppression – has given us

a dynamic account of language which sees it pulled in opposite directions: centripetally, towards the unitary centre provided by a notion of a 'national language'; and centrifugally, towards the various languages which actually constitute the apparent but false unity of a national language. (Dentith, 1995, p. 35)

Bakhtin coined the word 'heteroglossia' to describe the 'multiplicity of actual "languages" which are at any time spoken by the speakers of any "language"' (Dentith, 1995, p. 35) and which resist that pull towards the standardized, normative centre which a national language can exert. People who will not or cannot conform to the demands of the standard language risk marginalization and disempowerment. As Dentith observes:

if you are one of the world's population who speaks a non-prestige version of your 'national' language or indeed don't speak that language at all, you will know the sharp and sometimes bitterly conflictual tensions that surround every word you speak. (Dentith, 1995, p. 37)

The Nazis believed fundamentally in the supremacy of the 'unitary centre'. The demand for it is there right from the start of the movement – in the 25 point programme of 1920 cited earlier:

25. We demand: the creation of a strong central authority in the Reich. Unquestioned authority by the political central Parliament over the entire Reich and its organizations in general. (Landau, 1998, p. 59)

Bakhtin's concept of 'heteroglossia' would have been abhorrent to the Nazis. One of the things which Hitler most loathed about his time in Vienna, capital of the polyglot Habsburg empire, was its vibrant cultural and national mix:

Czechs, Poles, Hungarians, Ruthenians, Serbs and Croats ... and always the Jews, here and there and everywhere – the whole spectacle was repugnant to me. (Supple, 1992, p. 62)

To the Nazis, speaking a different or non-standard language could be a capital offence. This is Hitler in 1939, commenting on the invasion of Poland:

I have sent to the east ... My 'Death's Head Units', with the order to kill without mercy men, women and children of Polish race *or language* [my italics]. (Landau, 1998, p. 91)

THE POLITICAL DIMENSION

It is here, on the territory of language, that English teachers must initiate the counterattack against the forces which created the Holocaust. Many of the battles will be fought in the classroom, but there is one in particular which requires English teachers to enter the political arena beyond the school gates. The Nazis' insistence upon standardization, conformity, the equation between language and national identity, strikes disturbing resonances at the present day. Take the current situation in England as just one example. It would be interesting to hear what Bakhtin's response would have been to the idea of a legally enforceable National Curriculum which insisted that all students educated within the state system between the ages of 5 and 16 should be taught – and assessed through the medium of – something called 'Standard English' (Department for Education/ Welsh Office (DFE/WO), 1995). What Dentith describes as 'the powerful mythology that has been created around the prestige form of English spoken in England' (Dentith, 1995, p. 37) is reinforced by the privileging, within the National Curriculum, of a 'cultural heritage' approach to textual study: 'the one in which you can only study the works of English writers, born in England, writing in "standard" English and covering themes like tea on the lawn, croquet and being a butler' (Andrews, 1992, p. 11).

Richard Andrews exaggerates for comic effect, but not overmuch. Most of the National Curriculum's list of named authors recommended for study by students between the ages of 14 and 16 are dead white males. Not one of those named comes from outside the British Isles (Department of Education and Science/Welsh Office (DES/ WO), 1995, p. 20). Andrews' joke wears even thinner when one bears in mind the words of Ron Carter, a man who speaks with particular authority on the subject because he fronted a major government initiative on language in the English National Curriculum in the late 1980s (Carter, 1990). Speaking at the end of the project, Carter warns:

> English is synonymous with Englishness, that is, with an understanding of who the proper English are. A view of one English with a single set of rules accords with a monolingual, monocultural version of society intent on preserving an existing order in which everyone knows their place. (Carter, 1992, p. 3)

To read the statement which follows in the context of Carter's words is to feel a distinct sense of unease. It was issued by John Patten when he was Secretary of State for Education in John Major's Conservative government: 'The sooner children master the basic skills and become confident users of standard English ... the sooner ... they can ... enjoy the pleasures and rewards of our literature' (DES/WO, 1993, p. 71).

It is that little pronoun 'our' which causes the difficulty. Who does it include? Who does it exclude? Over whose literature does it claim possession? John Major himself had no difficulty in deciding who the chosen might be. Echoing, in April 1993, the words of George Orwell, he defined his vision of England thus: 'The long shadows falling across the county ground, the warm beer, the invincible green suburbs, dog lovers and pools fillers ... old maids bicycling to Holy Communion through the morning mist' (Atkinson, 1995, p. 3).

One high-ranking Conservative politician hinted at a connection between deviance from the normative, standardized language and criminal behaviour. Here is an extract from an interview he gave to national radio in November 1985:

> We've allowed so many standards to slip ... Teachers weren't bothering to teach kids to spell and to punctuate properly ... if you allow standards to slip to the stage where good English is no better than bad English, where students turn up filthy ... at school ... All those things tend to cause people to have no standards at all, and once you lose standards then there's no imperative to stay out of crime. (Bain, 1991, p. 12)

It is not my intention, in raising these issues, to denigrate the wonderful works of literature written by the authors named in the English National Curriculum document. Nor do I wish to hurl simplistic accusations of crypto-fascism at democratic, right-of-centre politicians who, according to their own lights, are expressing sincerely held concerns about the future of society. What I am saying, however, is that people who try to use language as a means of imposing conformity, of deciding who is and who is not fit to belong to this or that social grouping, are treading on very dangerous ground. It was with statements not very dissimilar to the ones quoted above that the Nazis began their attritional assault upon the consciousness of the German people. This is why present-day English teachers must mount a constant and vigilant guard upon the curriculum. Working through their professional organizations on a national and international level, they need to engage the policy-makers in political debate – not only by challenging their assertions and demands but also by actively seeking to set the agenda for educational reform. It is too easy to assume that the more-or-less-humane consensus which has prevailed in the teaching of English since 1945 (Mathieson, 1975; Cox, 1991) will last forever. To cite England as an example again, the Secretary of State for Education and Employment already possesses the statutory power to implement whatever curriculum he or she wishes. As John White has warned: 'A most powerful way of indoctrinating students is by so organizing their studies that certain kinds of reflection ... are off the agenda' (White, 1988, p. 62).

Who is to say what a future government might choose to remove from the educational agenda? In the words of Peter Medway: 'When practice changes in the English curriculum, the previous practice, hitherto taken as 'natural', is revealed as simply the instance that happened to be realized out of a set of possible alternatives' (Medway, 1991, p. 159). It is the duty of English teachers to make sure, through their vigilance, that the 'set of possible alternatives' is a righteous one.

CREATING AN ENVIRONMENT IN WHICH THE HOLOCAUST CAN BE TAUGHT

But what about teaching the Holocaust within the English classroom? That is, after all, the place where we spend most of our professional lives and where, as I said earlier, we will confront the issues on a daily basis. I believe that there are two approaches we can take. We can study the Holocaust itself through the medium of the English curriculum and we can attempt to eradicate the seeds from which that evil flowering grew. I make no apologies for examining the latter alternative first; for if we are to teach the Holocaust effectively, it is important that we create an environment in which the subject *can* be taught.

I tried to demonstrate, in the opening section of this chapter, how control of language, or – in Plato's phrase – supervision of 'the production of stories', played a powerful part in the Nazis' success. It follows then that one of the most effective ways of preventing the conditions which allowed the Holocaust to occur is to instil in our students that same 'feeling for words and for what they could do' which the English teacher, Mr Williams, displayed in Edward Blishen's classroom – and which the Nazis perverted so effectively – in the 1930s. Writing about the same time, the celebrated critic F.R. Leavis observed how the Nazis were rising upon the tide of their own propaganda:

> The social and cultural disintegration that has accompanied the development of the vast modern machine is destroying what should have been the control, and leaves a terrifying apparatus of propaganda ready to the hands of the more or less subtle, more or less conscious, more or less direct, emulators of Hitler and his accomplices. What is to forestall or check them? ... Without an intelligent, educated and morally responsible public, political programmes can do nothing to arrest the process of disintegration. (Leavis, 1943, p. 118)

The answer provided by Leavis and Thompson – their famous exhortation 'to discriminate and to resist' (Leavis and Thompson,

1942, p. 3) – still holds good at the turn of the century. The way we can do this is by creating a school environment in which Bakhtin's 'heteroglossia' is celebrated: one in which *all* voices – not just those of the strong, the authoritative and the extrovert – are valued and allowed to have their say. We must – in the words of the National Association for the Teaching of English (NATE) – allow 'as many voices as possible into the classroom' (NATE, 1988, p. 20).

How might English teachers translate principles into practice? One significant first step taken by colleagues who have attempted to address these issues is the establishment of a whole-school initiative designed to raise awareness of and increase respect for voices different from the standardized norm. Authoritative, attractively produced texts written in a variety of languages are displayed throughout the school, starting with a multilingual 'Welcome!' poster in the entrance hall and including examples drawn from literature, science and popular culture. Seemingly mundane information texts, such as signs indicating 'staffroom' or 'dining area', for example, are written in several languages – and not just the conventional choices of French, German and Spanish, but ones drawn from a wider range within and beyond the continent of Europe. Artists and guests from a variety of cultural and linguistic backgrounds are invited into school. Students whose mother tongue is not English are encouraged to speak about their home language proudly and authoritatively to teachers and peers in and outside of the classroom. The ability to speak in dialect as well as in Standard English is seen as an accomplishment rather than a problem.

A second strand of this particular initiative requires a rigorous appraisal of the way in which language itself is regarded throughout the school. To take talk as an example, what is the attitude to swearing in the corridors or the playground? Or to the casual verbal brutality – the name-calling, the sarcastic remarks, the snide comments – which people working under pressure in a closed environment can so readily inflict upon each other? Do students feel that they can bring the language of the home inside the school gates and use it as a legitimate medium for communication, self-expression and learning? During lessons, does every person – including the most shy and sensitive – feel that she or he has a right to speak their mind? Or is talk sanctioned and policed by an unsympathetic teacher? Or by a group of extrovert students from their 'high status' position in the back row of the classroom? Much emphasis is now laid in English lessons upon the internalizing of knowledge through the medium of 'process talk'. But what actually happens when a teacher sets up an exercise and utters the fateful instruction 'Get into groups'? Friend scrambles to be with friend, boy with boy, girl with girl. The shy and the unpopular look at their feet and wait for the teacher to complete their humiliation by allocating them to a group which did not voluntarily welcome them in. Yet it is in this apparently routine, day-to-day activity that the seeds of civic responsibility and democratic practice can be sown. In English classrooms where talk is well managed, teachers and students establish clear rules and opportunities for turn-taking and for sensitive listening. The principle that every person in the room can be expected to work in a professional manner with every other person is asserted as fundamental. Groups are carefully structured according to this principle. Specific roles – chairperson, scribe, spokesperson – are allocated to group members on a rotational basis so that everybody has a chance to experience the roles and responsibilities – the turn-taking, the arguing, the negotiating, the conceding, the listening – associated with democratic procedure. In such schools, teachers, too, think hard about the kinds of language they use with their students and with each other. They do not write terse, anonymous comments like 'Good' or 'Disappointing' on marked work; they use the name of the person they are addressing and they provide a sensitive personal response to what they have read. They do not talk about the groups they teach in blanket terms, such as 'Class 7A is stupid'. They do not resort to sarcasm as a controlling device in lessons. They communicate with colleagues in a professional manner which is free of bias.

These are cross-curricular initiatives which English teachers might initiate and encourage. Working in their own subject specialism, they can prepare an environment within which the Holocaust might be taught by placing the study of language at the heart of the curriculum. Postmodern critical theories, the revolution in electronic communication and the ever-increasing global influence of the visual and print media have brought a renewed interest in the ways in which language is constructed, mediated and received (Halliday, 1989, 1990; Carter, 1990; Andrews, 1992; Lanham, 1996). From their colleagues in media education, for example, English teachers might borrow the following set of so-called signpost questions which can be asked of any text:

- Who is communicating, and why?
- What type of text is it?
- How is it produced?
- How do we know what it means?
- Who receives it, and what sense do they make of it?
- How does it present its subject? (Bowker, 1991, p. 6)

To teach students how to subject texts to this kind of interrogation is to empower them with the capacity for discrimination and resistance which Leavis and Thompson (1942) advocated as a response to the threat of Nazism. The principle is put into practice wherever students are invited to analyse the ways in which texts of all kinds – be they adverts or newspapers or novels, for example – attempt to position and persuade an audience. Teachers concerned with working on the Holocaust are not faced here with the task of introducing an entirely new way of teaching. The weapons are already in place; they need to be redirected at a target older and more virulent than modern-day xenophobic tabloid headlines or insidiously persuasive television adverts.

TEACHING THE HOLOCAUST THROUGH ENGAGEMENT WITH TEXTS

One way, then, into teaching the Holocaust through the medium of the English curriculum is to challenge Nazi ideology directly by making its texts – the propaganda, government documents and the rest – the subject of focused language and media work in the classroom. Take the 1942 government memorandum 'Secret Reich Business' (quoted earlier) as an example:

> Since December 1941, ninety-seven thousand have been processed by the three vehicles in service, with no major incidents. In the light of observations made so far, however, the following technical changes are needed. (Landau, 1998, p. 35)

The sense of evil, of deviousness, of linguistic manipulation inherent in this text is exposed with forensic thoroughness by the 'signpost questions'. Ask of this document 'Who is communicating and why?' Our attention is drawn to the title with its equation of secrecy, imperialism and industrially organized genocide. The first adjective is particularly significant: it suggests that the communicators of this text must have had some sense of shame because they wanted the terrible things they were writing about to remain hidden from public scrutiny. The 'signpost' question forces them to reveal themselves: the bureaucrats prepared to turn their administrative skills to the business of murder as easily as, under another regime, they might have addressed issues of street-lighting or road maintenance; the powerful empire-builders who conceived of a state where the strong impose terror upon the weak. The list of 'communicators' implicated in this text widens. Who supplied the paper for it? Who set up the

typeface? Who printed and distributed it? Who thought it was
'normal' to use words in this way? The one 'signpost question'
provokes a sequence of other, equally disturbing, questions. They
need to be asked in the classroom because they raise profound issues
central to English teaching and therefore to our understanding of
what it means to be the citizen of a civilized state: what is the
relationship between language and authority? How do texts achieve
power and how is that power used? How can we read against texts
which seek to position us as powerless or even evil?

Each of the six 'signpost questions' is capable of inflicting this kind
of damage upon the authority of a text like 'Secret Reich Business'.
There is space here only for one more example. The answer to the
question 'How does this text present its subject?' requires a
specifically linguistic focus. One needs to be aware, for example,
that the text makes no use at all of the personal pronoun; that the
number 'ninety-seven thousand' is not followed by a noun. One can
ask how the verb 'processed' – with its connotations of the factory
conveyor belt – found its way into a text about murder. Discourse
markers play an important part here. The document is written in the
language of the bureaucrat – 'vehicles in service', 'no major
incidents', 'in the light of observations', 'the following technical
changes' – yet the subject is genocide. Unless English teachers give
their students the linguistic tools needed to deconstruct this text, its
authors might yet succeed in keeping their evil deeds secret from
future generations.

Having scrutinized the language of 'Secret Reich Business', one
can force its grotesque secrets out into the open by writing the real
text which is hiding behind the official version. This is how it might
read if we were to add the missing nouns and pronouns and take
away the euphemisms:

> Since December 1941, ninety-seven thousand men, women and children have
> been murdered in three mobile gas chambers, without any outbreaks of
> resistance which our guards could not control. Having watched the murders
> taking place, we would like to suggest ways in which the imprisonment of the
> victims in the gas chambers – and the act of choking them to death – might be
> made more efficient.

Place the two texts side by side and one must become aware at once
of the evil purposes to which language can be put: the justifying of
wickedness; the dehumanizing of enemies; the distancing of human
beings from the evil that they do. These are not comfortable tasks for
English teachers to set their students. It would be far easier to leave
them to the deconstruction of contemporary newspaper features or

television adverts. But unless we confront the texts of Nazism, unless we force them to say what they really mean, we cannot hope to know the enemy or to learn how to defeat it.

If it is important for English teachers to teach their students how to read 'against' the texts of Nazism, so it is equally important for those students to learn how to take to their hearts the texts of the Nazi's victims. Here, Jana Markoulova, a survivor of the Romany Holocaust, recounts the murder of her grandfather at the hands of Czech guards in the concentration camp at Lety, South Bohemia:

> My grandfather ... was also there. They asked him to bring water from the well. He had a pole across his shoulders to carry two buckets at a time. When he had the buckets full they beat him. Then they kicked him into the well. After he climbed out, they made him turn the wheel and bring up water again. Then they kicked him in again. They kept doing this until he drowned. I saw this with my own eyes. I was screaming. The guards had a lot of fun doing this.
> (Mortkowitz, 1998, p. B4)

Let us put to this text a third signpost question: 'Who receives it and what sense do they make of it?' Our first response might be to wish to distance ourselves from Jana Markoulova's words – for the best of motives. How can we hope to cross the gulf between the nightmare world she describes and the comparatively safe, familiar world of the classroom? To attempt to do so might seem like an act of impertinence. Yet it is essential that we make the effort. If we do not, we are in danger of doing the very thing the Nazis did – defining her as 'other' and placing her 'out there' in a space so remote from our own that the screams she describes might as well be coming at us soundlessly from behind a thick pane of glass. We have to look for connections. We do this by using a strategy learned from drama teachers. We feel for the pulse of this text. We focus and refine our gaze till we find its essence. At the heart of Jana Markoulova's text lies an account of what it feels like to be totally disempowered; to witness a monstrous act of injustice which you can do nothing to prevent; to watch helplessly as someone you love and revere is tortured to death. We hope profoundly that our students never have to experience what Jana Markoulova experienced as a child; yet we know that, although they are still young, they will already be able to relate, in some way, to some of the things she is talking about – the love of a grandparent, perhaps, or the fear of bullying (even as I write, a new report from the English Health Education Authority has revealed that half of all children have been bullied at school at some time: Judd, 1999).

Contemplating the atrocities committed in his troubled homeland, the Irish poet Seamus Heaney asked: 'How with this rage shall beauty hold a plea?' (Heaney, 1980, p. 57). Is it possible for English teachers to help their students find some kind of 'beauty' which might 'hold a plea' with the 'rage' of the Holocaust? Lanham (1996) has reaffirmed the Victorian novelist George Eliot's faith in the moral power of literature to extend our understanding of and empathy for lives beyond our own: 'it can be argued that we in fact grow not by continually thinking about ourselves, but in fact by playing other kinds of roles and learning to internalize them and understand them from the inside' (Lanham, 1996, p. 40).

I do not believe that we can ever dare to play the role of Holocaust victims in this way. Perhaps a more appropriate response lies in Seamus Heaney's answer to the question quoted earlier. Beauty, he said, can hold a plea with rage 'by offering "befitting emblems of adversity"'. We can make connections between Jana Markoulova's experience and our own, yes, by witnessing it first; but then by creating bridging metaphors between our two worlds. Let our students talk and write about their responses to Jana Markoulova's story; but let them, too, try to link their lives to hers by creating 'emblems' – through all the forms of communication at the disposal of the English teacher – of mourning, loss and love.

Let me close this chapter with an example of what I mean. This is a poem called 'September Song' written by the great English poet, Geoffrey Hill. I want to quote the poem in full and let the magnificent words speak for themselves. Before I do, I just ask you to consider four things: how the poem begins by gazing unflinchingly into the horror of the Holocaust; how its metaphorical 'emblems' of September and flaking roses answer the opening rage; how the adjective 'harmless' in the penultimate line explodes the poem with the force of a depth-charge; and finally, I ask you to commit the last line to memory.

September Song
born 19.6.32 – deported 24.9.42

Undesirable you may have been, untouchable
you were not. Not forgotten
or passed over at the proper time.

As estimated, you died. Things marched,
sufficient, to that end.
Just so much Zyklon and leather, patented
terror, so many routine cries.

(I have made
an elegy for myself it
is true)

September fattens on vines. Roses
flake from the wall. The smoke
of harmless fires drifts to my eyes.

This is plenty. This is more than enough.

(From 'September Song', from *Collected Poems* by Geoffrey
Hill, Penguin Books 1985, first published in King Log 1968.
Copyright © Geoffrey Hill 1968, 1985. Reproduced by
permission of Penguin Books Ltd)

REFERENCES

Andrews, R. (ed.) (1992) *Rebirth of Rhetoric: Essays in Language, Culture and Education*. London: Routledge.

Atkinson, J. (1995) How do we teach pre-twentieth century literature? In P. King and R. Protherough (eds) *The Challenge of the National Curriculum*. London: Routledge.

Bain, R. (1991) *Reflections: Talking about Language*. London: Hodder and Stoughton.

Blishen, E. (1978) *Sorry, Dad: An Autobiography*.   London: Hamish Hamilton.

Bowker, J. (ed.) (1991) *Secondary Media Education: A Curriculum Statement*. London: British Film Institute.

Carter, R. (ed.) (1990) *Knowledge about Language and the Curriculum: The LINC Reader*. London: Hodder and Stoughton.

Carter, R. (1992) The LINC Project: The Final Chapter? Text of speech, 22 February.

Cox, B. (1991) *Cox on Cox: An English Curriculum for the 1990s*. London: Hodder and Stoughton.

Dentith, S. (1995) *Bakhtinian Thought: An Introductory Reader*. London: Routledge.

Department of Education and Science/Welsh Office (DES/WO) (1993) *English for Ages 5 to 16*. London: HMSO.

Department for Education/Welsh Office (DFE/WO) (1995) *English in the National Curriculum*. London: HMSO.

Halliday, M.A.K. (1989) *Spoken and Written Language*. Oxford, Oxford: University Press.

Halliday, M.A.K. (1990) *Linguistic Perspectives on Literacy: A Systemic-Functional Approach*. Mimeo. Sydney: Department of Linguistics, University of Sydney.

Heaney, S. (1980) Feeling into words. In Heaney, *Preoccupations: Selected*

Prose 1968–1978. London: Faber and Faber.

Heimer, E. (1938) *The Poisonous Mushroom [Der Giftpilz]*. London.

Hill, G. (1968) September Song. In Hill, *King Log*. London: André Deutsch.

Judd, J. (1999) Students believe Pill can stop Aids, *Independent,* 13 March, 7.

Lanham, R. (1996) The electronic world: multimedia, rhetoric and English teaching. *English and Media Magazine*, 35, (autumn), 40–3.

Landau, R.S. (1998) *Studying the Holocaust: Issues, Readings and Documents*. London: Routledge.

Leavis, F.R. (1943) Why universities? In Leavis, *Education and the University: A Sketch for an 'English School'*. London: Chatto and Windus.

Leavis, F.R. and Thompson, D. (1942) *Culture and Environment*. London: Chatto and Windus.

Lee, D. (trans.) (1987) *Plato: The Republic*. Harmondsworth: Penguin.

Marrus, M. (1988) *The Holocaust in History*. London: Weidenfeld and Nicolson.

Mathieson, M. (1975) *The Preachers of Culture: A Study of English and its Teachers*. London: Allen and Unwin.

Medway, P. (1991) Modes of engagement through language, *Educational Review*, **43**(2), 159–69.

Mortkowitz, S. (1998) A grave silence: the voices of genocide, *The Prague Post,* 23–9 September, B4–B5.

National Association for the Teaching of English (NATE) Language and Gender Committee (1988) *Gender Issues in English Coursework*. Sheffield: NATE.

Supple, C. (1992) *From Prejudice to Genocide: Learning about the Holocaust*. Stoke-on-Trent: Trentham Books.

White, J. (1989) An unconstitutional National Curriculum. In L. Bash and D. Coulby (eds) *The Education Reform Act: Competition and Control*. London: Cassell.

Chapter 10

Teaching the Holocaust through History

Terry Haydn

DOING JUSTICE TO THE HOLOCAUST

'You're not going to show us more dead Jews are you sir?'

The Holocaust is a compulsory subject of study in the National Curriculum for England and Wales. Under the draft proposals for the revision of the National Curriculum for history, the Holocaust will be the *only* topic specified by name which will be a compulsory part of the history curriculum. This in itself will present opportunities for history teachers to get pupils to think about the Holocaust, in terms of a possible starting point for approaching the topic. Why has it been bequeathed such special status? Why is it deemed so important that all children in state schools must study it? Most history teachers feel a sense of responsibility when they teach the Holocaust, both to their subject, to the gravity of the topic and the memory of its victims. Most of us accept that we cannot always be successful in searing learning experiences in history into pupils' consciousness so that they will remember them for years, but most of us would like pupils to remember, and think about the Holocaust after the lesson has ended.

In some respects, the Holocaust is problematic and double-edged for history teachers. In his *Principles of History Teaching*, Burston (1963) pointed out that one of the central challenges facing the history teacher is to persuade the pupils of the relevance and importance of the past. Given the continuing high profile of the Holocaust in the media generally, it would seem to offer more possibilities in this respect than the wool trade in the fourteenth century, for example, or Renaissance architecture.

Against this is the teacher's dilemma about exactly what learning outcomes are desired from a study of the Holocaust, and how to achieve them. Like any other topic in history, the Holocaust can be well taught or badly taught. If we cannot do justice to a topic such as the Holocaust, what is the point of inflicting history on young people? One first step might be to think of the dangers and pitfalls which we would seek to avoid.

First, as subject experts in history, we must not take things for granted or make assumptions about pupils' knowledge and understanding about the Holocaust. Research has revealed that in Britain, France, Germany, Canada and the United States, substantial numbers of young people know little or nothing about the Holocaust; in some countries, almost one-third of young people doubt that the elimination of 6 million Jews ever took place (de Laine, 1997). Nor must we make assumptions about the feelings of young people about the Holocaust. The statement quoted at the top of this chapter was a comment made to a student teacher about to teach the topic. There have been instances of pupils laughing at footage of the concentration camps. As Linda Blackburne points out,

> Appalling though it must seem to most adults, the Holocaust is just another story to many young children today. To them, it's as distant as the Battle of Hastings or the Crusades. For some, not even their grandparents have memories of the Second World War. (Blackburne, 1995, p. 8)

Even if a solid grounding in the events of the Holocaust is established with pupils (and accepted by pupils to be true) there is still the important 'So what?' question, the danger that they might still say, or feel, 'What has this got to do with my life?' We must not assume that because, as teachers, we regard the Holocaust as an important issue, it appears in that light to our pupils. Many of the pupils we teach do not have an avid scholarly interest in finding out about the past. Sometimes we have to incorporate into our teaching methods strategies for drawing them into engagement with the past. Sometimes the best starting point in history is the present day rather than the distant past.

It is possible to teach the Holocaust as an unproblematic and straightforward event: at its worst, there was a wicked man called Hitler, who lived in Germany a long time ago, and built concentration camps where the Jews were rounded up and gassed. Eventually he lost the Second World War, killed himself, and many of those responsible for helping him were brought to trial and punished. If this seems a caricature, it is not entirely uncharacteristic of materials which are sometimes used to teach the Holocaust, such as 'Fill in the missing words' exercises: 'Hitler/6million/gassed/concentration-camps/MeinKampf/Holocaust/1942/slave labour' to give one example. Although this is not morally repellent in the same way as antisemitic Internet Holocaust denial sites, and might be considered better than nothing, this approach misses some of the important opportunities which the topic presents. Similar problems arise with an approach which focuses primarily on the concentration camps, and uses resources which highlight pictures of piles of corpses and statistics of victims. It helps to answer some questions about the Holocaust – what happened to the Jews, the scale of the death camps – but leaves many other questions we might ask about the Holocaust unaddressed. The belief that pupils should know what happened, that it was wrong and that it should not happen to anyone else, is understandable, but still leaves important aspects of the Holocaust unexplored; it is history with the thinking taken out. As the United States Holocaust Memorial Museum website points out, 'We must avoid simple answers to complex history' (ushmm.org/education/guidelines.html)

This is not a matter of moral relativism, but of subjecting sources of information about the Holocaust to the same questions which we would ask of other historical events. So instead of 'This is what happened; wasn't it terrible?' we need to ask the usual general range of questions which the discipline of history requires, while remembering that there are differences between the purposes of academic history, and the purposes of teaching history to young people. We need to get beyond approach A, and towards approach B:

This is what happened; wasn't it terrible?	What happened, and how do we find out about it?
	Why are there different accounts and explanations?
	How do we find out which accounts and explanations are most valid? (Which can we trust?)
	Why does it matter and why is it important?
	In what way does this affect the present and the future; what light does it shed on current problems and issues?

If by exploring these questions with relation to the Holocaust, we fail to convince pupils that the same questions and issues which gave rise to the Holocaust will have a significant influence on all of their lives, and that the Holocaust was not just something that happened over half a century ago which has nothing much to do with them, we will have failed to do justice to the Holocaust, and to its victims.

WHAT QUESTIONS DO WE ASK?

Teaching an aspect of history is in some ways like being given a piece of raw meat to prepare, in the sense that the teacher needs to think of exactly what to do with the raw materials of the past. The National Curriculum for History in England and Wales asks (among other things) that pupils should learn to

- assess the significance of events
- describe, analyse and explain reasons for and results of historical events
- make links between different events and areas of study
- understand how and why some events have been interpreted differently
- analyse and evaluate interpretations
- investigate independently aspects of periods studied
- ask and answer significant questions.

History teachers are also asked to take advantage of opportunities to contribute to pupils' moral, spiritual, cultural and social development.

Study of the Holocaust could address all of these elements in the development of pupils' historical knowledge and understanding. The extent to which the various stands are explored will depend on the age of the pupils concerned, and the amount of time available, but at all ages, it is helpful if teachers try to develop the learners' understanding of history as a form of knowledge as well as a body of knowledge. (For further development of this important point, see Lee, 1994.)

If we simply transmit a received account of the Holocaust, and 'preach' about the wickedness of Hitler and the iniquity of the values and policies which led to the Holocaust, are we equipping pupils with the intellectual foundations that will enable them to subject contemporary values and policies to intelligent scrutiny? 'As Lord Lane remarked, "Oppression does not stand on the doorstep with a toothbrush moustache and a swastika armband. It creeps up insidiously, step by step"' (quoted in Supple, 1994). As well as providing a foundation of knowledge about what happened and how it has been explained, we need to teach the Holocaust in a way which develops pupils' ability to handle and decode information intelligently. More than with most topics, we want pupils to think further about the Holocaust, outside the history classroom, and to cross-reference it to contemporary events. We are more likely to achieve this by getting pupils to think about the problems and complexities of interpreting the events of the Holocaust, rather than presenting it as a simple and unproblematic narrative.

There are a range of questions we can ask about the Holocaust, and a range of teaching strategies to explore them; but we are more likely to elicit genuine engagement and profound thinking if we ask difficult questions about the Holocaust rather than easy ones, in the same way that the American educator, Lawrence Kohlberg (1984) used discussion of moral dilemmas to cultivate the moral and ethical development of young people. Such questions might include:

- Is the Holocaust 'special' or different in some way from other events in history; if so why, what is its significance?
- When did it start?
- To what extent was Hitler to blame for the Holocaust?
- To what extent was it about Germany and German history?
- To what extent is the Holocaust about the Jews?
- Why didn't other countries do more to stop it?
- Why did ordinary 'educated' people do terrible things?
- To what extent was it unique or different from other genocides?
- To what extent was it about eugenics and 'the efficient society', and what messages does that have for us today?
- How can people deny the Holocaust when there is so much evidence to support it?
- Should it be illegal to deny the Holocaust?
- What does the Holocaust tell us about human nature and the human spirit?
- Are some questions about the Holocaust more important than others?

I do not claim that this list is comprehensive; what the questions have in common is that to at least some degree, there are different views on them. These can be used to problematize the Holocaust; to get pupils to think about it, in its own right, and with reference to some of the choices they may have to make which mirror those made by those involved in the Holocaust itself. Part of this is to get the pupils to think beyond the concentration camps and the gas chambers. If we cannot do that, we will limit their understanding of what happened, and why it matters to the lives they will lead.

TEACHING APPROACHES

The importance of narrative

Laurillard (1999) and others have stressed the importance of providing a narrative that will provide orientation for learners as they explore conceptual and philosophical aspects of history, but pupils do need to know *more* than just what happened, if they are to make sense of the Holocaust and the issues it raises.

Many history departments adopt a self-consciously different approach to the Holocaust, in order to stress its importance. One strategy which has been used by several schools is to show the Holocaust episode of Thames Television's *World at War* (Thames video, 1974) documentary to pupils, as a whole lesson without any pre- or post-screening commentary or questioning by the teacher. There is no music at the start or end of the one-hour documentary, and pupils are (in some schools) asked to walk into and out of the room in silence, in order to show respect for the victims. It has been argued that this approach is suitable only for older pupils. The aspiration is that in the (unusual) absence of teacher explanation and questioning, pupils will be more inclined to continue to think about the issues raised by the programme outside the classroom, and that the departure from usual lesson format will help to engrave the experience into their consciousness.

Another strategy widely used in British classrooms is the use of Holocaust survivors to tell pupils of their experiences, from the start of their persecution to the end of the war. All the student teachers I work with who have witnessed this approach speak in very positive terms of its impact and effectiveness. One example involved two Dutch survivors who talked of how it felt having to wear the star, of the lists drawn up for deportation and the common knowledge of what that entailed, of the narrow escapes and instances of good and bad fortune over the course of the war. The history student who observed this spoke of the (untypically) exemplary behaviour and engagement of the pupils, the commitment of pupils who had hitherto been profoundly disengaged in history, and of the sincerity and earnestness of their questioning. Both these approaches seemed to have the advantage of leaving the pupils wanting to find out more about the Holocaust, and talking about it after the end of the lesson –

and with others who had not been in the lesson; surely one of the outcomes we would hope for.

Other teachers have spoken of the importance of disturbing pupils' preconceptions that the Holocaust started with the concentration camps, as soon as Hitler came to power. The provision of a narrative enables teachers to make important points about progression in the treatment of the Jews, the ways in which the Nazis were sometimes sensitive to public opinion, and that not all Germans accepted policy towards the Jews unquestioningly. A Perspectives on the Holocaust conference (Islington and East London College, 17–18 March 1993) stressed the importance of giving pupils access to a chronology of the Holocaust, so that they could refer back to events as they explored some of the debates which later teaching addressed. A common starting point is 1933 – in itself an act of historical interpretation, which raises the question of whether the Holocaust was the sole responsibility of Nazism. Older pupils may be invited to explore in more depth the propositions that the Holocaust began many years before the Nazis came to power, and that it evolved out of a European rather than purely German tradition of antisemitism.

In addition to a prominently displayed chronology of events, classroom display maps are used to make explicit to pupils the scale and duration of the Holocaust. This is frequently complemented by biographical details of key figures in the Holocaust, often prepared by the pupils themselves as research activities. The maps produced made a deliberate attempt to extend students' awareness and knowledge of the Holocaust beyond the number of Jews who were killed by the Nazis. Maps can include details of massacres, pogroms and emigration between 1600 and 1920, the destinations of Jewish refugees between 1933 and 1945, with details of immigration regulations for the countries involved, German planning maps from the Wannsee Conference, the location of the labour and death camps, a map giving details of non-Jewish victims of Nazi rule, and details of Jewish revolts, 1942–5.

Stories to complement sources

In recent years, history teaching in England and Wales has moved towards an emphasis on skills-based learning and the critical examination of historical sources. The use of stories and biographies is one way of restoring the balance between overviews of events, and the close examination of historical detail. It also helps to remind pupils that history is about real people who lived, suffered and died (and who in some cases survived and triumphed). Biographies and stories provide another potential form of narrative, which can also offer the advantage of exploring different perspectives on the Holocaust, and ensuring that we do not only learn about the Holocaust from the perspectives of its victims. Many of the guides who show visitors round Auschwitz recommend that visitors should read the diaries and memoirs of SS guards rather than those of Jewish survivors as the best way of developing their understanding of the Holocaust (see, for instance, *KL Auschwitz seen by the SS* (published by the Auschwitz-Birkenau State Museum, Oświęcim, 1995), which contains the autobiography, reminiscences and diaries of Hoss, Broad and Kremer). One helpful development in terms of the integration of biography and story into teaching and learning is the move towards review and summary of nearly all recent research and publication on the Holocaust in newspapers, journals and television programmes. Television programmes on aspects of the Holocaust are also often cross-reported in newspapers in the form of reviews or short articles, which means that there is a fairly regular supply of manageable information about contemporary controversy and new findings on the Holocaust. This makes it easier to connect the Holocaust to the present in a way that helps to persuade pupils of its relevance to their lives. Some examples are briefly described in the next section. This is not to say that history teachers should not make use of academic studies still emerging on the Holocaust – it is part of their professional responsibility to keep up to date with scholarship and research in their subject – but this does require time and thought in terms of how to present a digest of them, given constraints on teaching time. The subcontracting of sources shedding light on different aspect of the Holocaust, to pupils who are then asked to report back to the whole class, can help to cover more ground in the time available.

'THE CLOSER YOU GET TO INDIVIDUAL EXPERIENCES, THE CLEARER THINGS BECOME' (GILBERT, 1992)

While there is a place for making points about the scale of the Holocaust, stories and anecdotes about individuals (significant or ordinary) whose lives were affected by the Holocaust can help to dispel stereotypes (all Germans were in the SS, all Jews were victims) and provide insight into a wide range of the questions posed in the previous section. They can also help to move pupils closer to an understanding of Arendt's (1979) articulation of 'the banality of evil', and away from Hollywood images of the Holocaust. In a talk about the work of the historian, Gilbert (1992) described the testimony of SS guards at Landau, with their emphasis on the tedium and poor quarters, 'pay, food, hours, slackers', and the comment of one guard, 'The work itself is not unpleasant.'

Gilbert also described the resistance of some middle-ranking German officers to the early executions, the moratorium and change of location of the killings, occasioned by protest and disquiet, and the court martial of a German soldier who refused to execute Jews, and his acquittal because no one could find the order in writing. Gilbert also described the pride of the official in charge of the Austrian railway network, who he interviewed some years after the war, in showing him the certificate from the SS for millions of deutschmarks, which had been negotiated by reclassifying extradited Jews as 'livestock' rather than 'freight of no commercial value'.

It has been claimed that the most cited extract from Anne Frank's diary is the statement that 'in spite of everything, I still believe that people are good at heart' (Karpf, 1999). Karpf suggests that the Holocaust has been hi-jacked by those who want their Holocaust stories to be about the triumph of the human spirit over evil and adversity. The study of a range of individual experiences from the Holocaust enables history teachers to present pupils with important questions about the human spirit, and human nature, rather than simply being supplied with all the answers, and not required to think. This can be a way of helping pupils to understand why such terrible things were allowed to happen, and why 'ordinary', 'educated', and 'civilised' people were often in some ways complicit in the events of the Holocaust (and are complicit in more modern tragedies today). It is reasonable for pupils to be told about W. Tym Miejscu and Maksymillian-Maria Kolbe, who volunteered to take the place of others condemned to die at Auschwitz, but they must also be asked to consider the full spectrum of responses to the human dilemmas which were posed by the Holocaust, including the gratuitous and casual infliction of harm described in the work of Goldhagen (1996), Browning (1993) and others.

ASSIGNING SIGNIFICANCE TO THE HOLOCAUST

The above approaches all tend to be teacher led, even though the aim of many of them is to draw pupils into active engagement with the questions posed by the Holocaust. Another way of developing pupils' understanding of the Holocaust is to ask them to evaluate its significance. It is often helpful to ask them about their prior knowledge and beliefs about the Holocaust at the start of the teaching sessions, and discuss significance at the end of the sessions, after the pupils have experienced a range of viewpoints and sources. Hunt's (1999) work on teaching pupils about significance makes the point that we should help pupils to understand that history operates on the basis that some events and changes are more important than others, and that they need to establish criteria for ascribing significance. He uses Partington's (1980) suggested criteria for assigning significance to events, to help pupils in discussing significance:

1. Importance – how important was it judged to be by people at the time?
2. Profundity – how deeply were people's lives affected?
3. Quantity – how many lives were affected?
4. Durability- for how long have people's lives been affected?
5. Relevance – in terms of the increased understanding of present life. (Partington, 1980, pp. 112–16)

One of Hunt's suggestions for getting pupils to think about significance is to present them with Partington's list, and a list of historical events, asking them to place them in order of their significance and explain the reasons for their choices. This could be done by either presenting the Holocaust as one of several events in twentieth-century history, or by placing it with other events within the Second World War. Pupils might also be asked to consider why the names of Auschwitz and Belsen are more widely known than those of Norilsk and Magadan, Soviet labour camps where vast numbers also perished through state persecution.

'SHARING THE HOLOCAUST'

I never saw a single German uniform when they took us away. (French Jewish deportee, quoted in *Guardian*, 18 February 1997)

Although Gilbert (1986) describes the Holocaust as 'The Jewish tragedy', the rationale behind the extermination of the Jews was based on eugenic theory, and the belief in the creation of the efficient society/state/nation. Many other groups, including homosexuals, Negroes, travellers, Slavs and mentally and physically handicapped people, were persecuted and killed. While not distorting the fact that the Jews bore the brunt of these policies, and were overwhelmingly the most affected group, drawing pupils' attention to the eugenic aspect of Hitler's policies enables us to explore a wider range of pertinent questions about the Holocaust. The treatment of people with disabilities and others deemed to be 'not useful to the state' in the Holocaust raises important questions about current social policy and philosophies of resource allocation which will impact on the lives of all our pupils. Is it possible to value people differently yet treat them equally?

Another aspect of sharing the Holocaust is the question of sharing responsibility for it, not just between Hitler and the Germans, but in terms of the moral responsibility of others involved in the Holocaust, in other countries. One could also explore the record of several other countries with regard to their own experiments with eugenics, and to their collusion with perpetrators of the Holocaust who were in some way useful. As in other aspects of the Holocaust, I have found newspaper articles to be a valuable resource in terms of providing useful sources on the responsibility and collusion of both governments and ordinary people (and the difficult dilemmas they faced) outside Germany. Broadening the scope of the Holocaust beyond the camps and the gas chambers makes it easier for us to explore the wide range of factors which led ordinary people to passively or actively collude in the Holocaust – selfishness, racism, obedience, indoctrination, the brutality of war? This helps to develop pupils' understanding of how it could have happened, and how similar things might happen today and in the future.

MAKING CONNECTIONS WITH THE HOLOCAUST

To be honest, with this sort of kit I tend not to ask too many questions about what they're doing with it ... As far as I'm concerned, they're grown men, they know what they're doing. (British salesman of electronic torture equipment, quoted on *Dispatches*, Channel 4 Television, 12 January 1995)

When Gilbert (1992) was asked when he thought the Holocaust began, he answered, 'The day that the Jews started to be treated differently'. Governments in many countries today are already treating groups of people differently, according to their perceived value to society. Warnings are being made about 'the threat to society from immoral people of low intelligence' (*Guardian*, 23 December 1996). Eugenics is not dead and has not gone away; Steinburg's (1995) review of Herrnstein and Murray's (1994) influential book, *The Bell Curve: Intelligence and Class Structure in American Life*, notes its message: 'The recipes for social policy become bleak. Don't waste money educating those of low cognitive ability. Don't provide state welfare: it only encourages low ability women to bear low ability babies' (Steinburg, 1995).

There is also the difficult (but historically valid) question of the uniqueness of the Holocaust in the light of other twentieth-century genocides. It could be argued that as in the 1930s and 1940s, international response to contemporary genocides is to at least some extent conditioned by economic, strategic and geographical considerations rather than moral ones. Might this not help pupils to understand why the Holocaust happened, and why some version of it might happen again?

If we want to persuade pupils of the importance of the Holocaust, we need to make connections with the present. As well as knowing what happened in the past, young people need to be aware that the questions we ask of the Holocaust are relevant to many of the complex human problems and dilemmas of the present day and will affect their lives and the world they grow up in.

RESOURCES

I have found both the Internet and the national press to be rich sources of eclectic, powerful and thought-provoking teaching materials. A useful starting point of reference for the Holocaust is the Cybrary of the Holocaust (http://www.remember.org). Resources include 'A chance dialogue with a contemporary Nazi' (http://www.remember.org/educate/munn.html), '60 Rightist lies and how to counter them' (http://www.remember.org/ideas/kz.html) and 'Teaching the Holocaust: Grades 4–12' (http://www.remember.org/educate/moretta.html). There are many other materials. The Chatback Trust offers the opportunity to provide pupils with 'virtual' oral history of the Holocaust by talking to members of the 'panel of elders'. (http://www.rmplc.co.uk/eduweb/sites/chatback). The US Holocaust Memorial Museum website provides a very helpful 'Guidelines for Teaching' section (http://www.ushmm.org/index.html).

Scarcely a month goes by when I don't come across a usable article from the newspapers. Three that I have found helpful to use with students are 'Judaism's witness: interview/biography of Thomas Buergenthal, survivor and Chair of the Committee of Conscience of the Holocaust Memorial Museum' (*Observer Magazine*, 4 April 1999), an article from the Imperial War Museum about lipstick in Belsen after the liberation (*Guardian*, The Editor section, 13 June 1998) and an article by Nicki Gerrard which relates Milgrims's experiment on obedience to authority to the massacre conducted by Battalion 101 of the German Reserve Police ('good family men') in Jozefow, Poland in 1942 (*Observer*, 12 October 1997).

Other excellent information technology resources are the *Lest we forget* CD-ROM (Logos Research systems) and the database *Mentor* (Actis software) in which the section on Hitler's Germany has an excellent selection of documents showing the progression in the treatment of the Jews in Germany from 1933 onwards (see Document A).

Document A

A mentally handicapped person costs the public 4 reichmarks per day, a cripple 5.50 reichmarks and a convicted criminal 3.50 reichmarks. Cautious estimates state that in Germany, 300,000 persons are being cared for in public mental institutions. How many marriage loans at 1,000 reichmarks per couple could be financed from funds allocated to such institutions? (An arithmetic problem from a German maths textbook, 1936: document from *Mentor* database)

There is a massive amount of video footage available. I have found material which goes beyond the camps and the gas chambers to be helpful; material on Holocaust museums raises interesting issues, as does Nazi footage of the camps, and extracts which focus on eugenics rather than Nazi policy. All secondary schools in England and Wales were issued with a copy of Spielberg's film, *Schindler's List*. The United States Holocaust Museum website contains a videography of Holocaust resources. Specialist teaching packs are available from the Holocaust Educational Trust (*Lessons of the Holocaust*) and from York City Council (*Anne Frank, A History for Today: Beliefs, Racism and Prejudice*).

I have found that simple quotations, left on classroom walls or presented as overhead transparencies, without comment, are a way of getting pupils to think about issues arising from the Holocaust. The first of these (Document B) is written by the headteacher of an inner-city school in New York and is given to teachers starting work at the school. The second is a reader's letter to the *Guardian* in response to the controversy over the views of Charles Murray on race and intelligence (Document C). I believe that the teaching of history can help young people to become wise about the Holocaust – understanding the complexity and breadth of questions it poses, and its relevance to their lives, rather than simply clever – in the sense of knowing what happened. Do we want to live in a society that values wisdom or cleverness?

Document B

Dear Teacher,

I am a survivor of a concentration camp. My eyes saw what no man should witness:

Gas chambers built by learned engineers.

Children poisoned by educated physicians.

Infants killed by trained nurses.

Women and babies shot and burned by high school and college graduates.

So, I am suspicious of education.

My request is: help your students become human. Your efforts must never produce learned monsters, skilled psychopaths, educated Eichmanns.

Reading, writing, arithmetic are important only if they serve to make our children more human.

Document C

Intelligence *per se* is neither good or bad. The use one makes of it is what is important. Wisdom is more valuable than intelligence, and Africans may have more of it.

It is better for people to be good and wise than to be clever, because if they are clever and bad, they can do a great deal of harm; whereas if they are good and wise, they never will, whether they are clever or not. (Simon Crawley, Stockport, *Guardian* 19 October 1994)

REFERENCES

Arendt, H. (1979) *Eichmann in Jerusalem: A Report on the Banality of Evil.* Harmondsworth: Penguin.

Blackburne, L. (1995) 'Oh what a moral war', *The Times Educational Supplement*, 5 May.

Browning, C. (1993) *Ordinary Men: Reserve Battalion 101 and the Final Solution in Poland.* New York: HarperCollins.

Burston, H. (1963) *Principles of History Teaching.* London: Methuen.

De Laine, M. (1997) 'Third of teenagers deny Holocaust', *Times Educational Supplement*, 4 July.

Gilbert, M. (1986) *The Holocaust: The Jewish Tragedy.* London: Collins.

Gilbert, M. (1992) The historian at work. Unpublished talk, Institute of Education, University of London, 10 December.

Goldhagen, D. (1996) *Hitler's Willing Executioners: Ordinary Germans and the Holocaust.* New York: Abacus.

Herrnstein, R. and Murray, C (1994) *The Bell Curve: Intelligence and Class Structure in American Life.* New York: Free Press.

Hunt, M. (1999) Teaching about significance in history. In J. Arthur and P. Phillips (eds), *Issues in History Teaching.* London: Routledge.

Laurillard, D. (1998) 'Multimedia and the learner's experience of narrative', *Computers in Education* **31**(2), 229–42.

Karpf, A. (1999) 'Let's pretend life is beautiful', *Guardian*, 3 April.

Kohlberg, L. (1984) *The Psychology of Moral Development: The Nature and Validity of Moral Stages.* London: Harper and Row.

Lee, P. (1994) Historical knowledge and the National Curriculum. In H. Bourdillon (ed.) *Teaching History.* London: Routledge.

Partington, G. (1980) *The Idea of an Historical Education*. Slough: National Foundation for Educational Research.
Steinburg (1995) 'Haves and have nots', *The Times Educational Supplement*, 27 January.
Supple, C. (1994) 'Teaching about the Holocaust', *Citizenship*, 3(2), 27–8.

Chapter 11

Teaching the Holocaust through Religious Education

Sue Foster and Carrie Mercier

This chapter examines the opportunities and the issues that are specific to or distinctive of an approach to the Holocaust that begins from within religious education, although some reference to opportunities for cross-curricular work will be made in the conclusion to the chapter.

Religious education is not part of the National Curriculum in England and Wales; it is part of what is called the basic curriculum and is required by the law in all schools. The syllabus for religious education is decided at local level and each LEA has its own guidelines for teaching the subject. This means that the opportunities for teaching about the Holocaust in religious education may vary from one LEA to another. The locally agreed syllabuses for religious education in schools require pupils to look at the major religious traditions and usually six are named – Christianity, Judaism, Islam, Hinduism, Buddhism and Sikhism. Teaching about the Holocaust in RE may come within a unit of work on Judaism in the first few years of secondary school. In many locally agreed syllabuses the Holocaust appears later in the RE programme and may be located within a unit of work on suffering and evil. This is the case for example in the agreed syllabus guidelines for LEAs London Borough of Croydon (1992, p. 24) and Manchester City Council Education Department (1996, p. 3). In other syllabuses the Holocaust is linked to social and moral issues within a scheme of work on prejudice or racism.

Many locally agreed syllabuses for religious education are now following, or are greatly influenced by the QCA (1998) *Model Syllabuses for Religious Education*, which were drawn up as a framework for locally agreed syllabuses in England and Wales. In these syllabuses we find the Holocaust listed under Judaism in a unit for pupils in the 14–16 age range which looks at 'the difficulty of maintaining traditional values in the modern world' (QCA, 1998, p. 55). Included in these guidelines are examples of questions to raise. One of the questions suggested for work on the Holocaust is 'Where was God and where was humanity?' This comes into the study of Judaism under the section on the 'application of Torah and Rabbinic principles in resolving contemporary issues' (QCA, 1998, p. 55). Given the influence of the QCA model syllabuses, it is likely that in a number of schools this will become the general pattern for teaching about the Holocaust in religious education. Teaching about the Holocaust is recognized by many as having a place within a programme of religious education in schools.

In some ways education in the UK is unique in providing a context for Holocaust teaching within a programme of religious education. In schools in the USA and in most European countries religion may be a focus in social studies, and schools with a religious foundation may have lessons of religious instruction but there is no established place for RE as in the UK. In this chapter we therefore want to ask what is distinctive about approaching the subject in RE? To follow this question we may be inclined to ask to what extent does teaching and learning about the Holocaust benefit from an approach within the context of religious education?

In establishing learning outcomes or objectives in any area of the curriculum, teachers are looking for knowledge and understanding of key concepts and the development of certain skills and attitudes. In religious education students are expected to develop their understanding of important religious concepts. The locally agreed syllabus will give guidance to teachers on key concepts for each world religion as well as on general concepts that cross the boundaries of the different faiths. Within a programme of study on Christianity, for example, the concepts of grace, sin, salvation and resurrection might be listed and within Judaism, the concepts of covenant, Torah, kosher and Shoah/Holocaust would be included. General concepts in RE would include for example the sacred or holy, revelation, worship, ritual, thanksgiving, sin and forgiveness.

In planning for teaching and learning about the Holocaust, RE teachers will identify both specific and general concepts that they will want their students to understand in approaching the subject through

RE. In terms of general concepts, one that will demand attention in religious education is the nature of evil and RE teachers in many secondary schools look at the Holocaust in a scheme of work on evil and suffering. In some schools this will include a comparison of the ways in which different religious traditions explain and respond to the problem of evil. The Holocaust is an appropriate area of concern in the examination of the problem of evil since the scale of the suffering and the nature of the evil raise important questions about the origins of evil. Teachers in history and social studies as well as RE encourage students to consider how so much evil could come about and reflect on who was responsible. The question often asked is whether it was the result of the evil intentions of one man or the indifference of the majority. In religious education there is another question, and that is how the Christian or the Jewish believer can accept a belief in a God who is all loving and all powerful in the face of so much evil and suffering. For many religious men and women the experience of the Holocaust was too great a test for their faith and RE teachers sometimes use the words of Elie Wiesel to explore this issue:

> Never shall I forget that night, the first night in the camp, which has turned my life into one long night, seven times cursed and seven times sealed. Never shall I forget that smoke. Never shall I forget the little faces of the children, whose bodies I saw turned into wreaths of smoke beneath a silent blue sky.
> Never shall I forget those flames which consumed my faith forever.
> Never shall I forget that nocturnal silence which deprived me for all eternity of the desire to live.
> Never shall I forget those moments which murdered my God and my soul and turned my dreams to dust.
> Never shall I forget these things, even if I am condemned to live as long as God himself. Never. (Bayfield, 1981, p. 182)

In answer to the question 'Where was God?', which is one of the key questions for RE, the only conclusion that some were able to come to was that there is no God. Others, like Rabbi Hugo Gryn, have argued that the Holocaust is no reason to reject God for he was not to blame: 'God did not put the Jews into Auschwitz, man did' (Supple, 1992, p. 266). The scale of the evil and the suffering in the events of the Holocaust raises disturbing questions for all humankind and these will be raised in history lessons as well as in religious education. However, there are particular issues raised by the events of the Holocaust for religious belief at the present time and for the individual believer. Secondary school students in religious education should be able to reflect on the place of religious faith in the light of the suffering and the evil encountered in the events of the Holocaust.

Another important concept that many RE teachers look at in the context of the Holocaust is the concept of forgiveness. Having looked at the events and the suffering, the question arises 'Where do we go from here: can there be forgiveness and reconciliation after such evil and suffering has been inflicted by one group of people on another?' The history lesson may raise the question of how there can be justice for those who have suffered and how the persecutors should pay for the evil they have done. However, it is unlikely that a history lesson or social studies lesson would have as the learning outcome or objective 'to understand the concept of forgiveness and to reflect on its meaning in the context of the Jewish experience of the Holocaust'. This is where religious education has a unique contribution to make in a programme of teaching and learning about the Holocaust. For example, students can reflect on the words of the prayer now found in the Chapel of the Holy Innocents in Norwich and the nature of the faith which inspired such forgiveness:

> O Lord, remember not only the men and women of goodwill, but also those of ill will. But do not remember all the suffering they have inflicted upon us; remember the fruits we have borne, thanks to this suffering; our comradeship, our loyalty, our humility, the courage, the generosity, the greatness of heart which has grown out of this and when they come to judgement, let all the fruits that we have borne be their forgiveness. Amen. (Written on a piece of wrapping paper, near the body of a dead child, at Ravensbruck)

In looking at the expressions of faith in the face of the Holocaust, students are enabled to draw on a wider range of experiences and responses in their own search for a way through the Holocaust story. Many students who look at the events of the Holocaust are deeply disturbed by the sense of human frailty in the face of fear and human guilt – and a nagging question hangs over us all – would I have done the same given the same circumstances, would I have said nothing and turned a blind eye? It is important in teaching young people about the Holocaust, that there is a balanced approach – between, on the one hand, the sense of horror at the evil of which human beings are capable and, on the other, a sense of wonder at the achievement of the human spirit – which, even in the face of terrible evil and suffering, can find the power to forgive. There are, of course, important questions about who has the right to say we should forgive and whether it is right to forgive and forget? Concepts such as forgiveness and reconciliation have a natural place in a programme of religious education and they demand a place in the teaching and learning about the Holocaust. A balanced approach is essential to building up the students' personal resources for responding at different levels to the story of Holocaust.

An important and relevant concept that RE teachers will want to explore in looking at the Holocaust is that of religious persecution. From the Jewish perspective, the Holocaust takes its place within a long history of persecution. This story of persecution is reflected in many of the holy days of the Jewish year. Students who are already familiar with the Jewish calendar of festivals will have gained some background knowledge of this history of religious persecution. At the festival of Purim, for example, Jews remember and celebrate the overthrow of a much earlier attempt at the extermination of the Jewish people during the reign of Queen Esther. At the popular festival of Hanukkah, Jews remember the time of religious persecution under the Syrians when the temple was desecrated. On the ninth day of Av called Tisha B'Av, Jews look back to two occasions when the temple in Jerusalem was destroyed and when Jewish lives were lost for the sake of the faith. On this occasion Jews read the Book of Lamentations and the day is regarded as a day of mourning. In secondary schools, the issue of persecution and, in particular, the persecution of minorities may appear in history or in social studies. However, the problem of religious persecution raises some important and difficult issues that are different from those raised in relation to the persecution of minorities in general. In many programmes of study on the Holocaust, students look at the centuries of religious persecution that came to fruition in the terrible events of the Holocaust. In the light of this history they can reflect on the experience facing people now who, on the one hand, hold strong religious convictions, while on the other recognize the rights of their neighbours to believe differently. These issues lead on to the challenging question of how to develop positive relations between the different faith communities in our society. The nature and value of dialogue between people of different religious traditions and the difficulties involved is an important issue for our young people to reflect on. Perhaps the most challenging issues arise when students are invited to consider the problems that religious communities come up against on occasions when religious commitments and traditions conflict with national law or matters to do with human rights. These issues which relate specifically to the problem of religious persecution should be an essential part of any programme of religious education and through examining the part played by religious persecution in the events of the Holocaust some of these very difficult issues are given a sharper focus.

Religious education not only involves understanding certain

concepts but also involves developing a range of skills. Many of the skills listed for religious education are ones that the teacher might expect to develop in other areas of the curriculum, for example we find the following skills described: 'Investigation – this includes asking relevant questions; knowing how to use different types of resources; Analysis – this includes distinguishing between opinion, belief and fact' (QCA, 1998, p. 5). There are also some skills listed that might be considered specific to RE, for example: 'Interpretation – this includes the ability to interpret religious language and religious ritual; Reflection – this includes the ability to reflect on feelings, relationships, experience, ultimate questions, beliefs and practices' (QCA, 1998, p. 5). Some of these skills will be regarded as important in setting learning outcomes for lessons on the Holocaust in religious education. In the light of the events of the Holocaust, many Jewish rituals and festivals have taken on new meaning and significance. Teachers can enable students to develop the skills needed to interpret the meaning of these rituals as they might be understood before and after the Holocaust. In this way they are able to gain insight into the nature of religious symbolism and ritual and the different levels of meaning with which they work. For example, the festival of Shabbat is an important subject to look at in any programme of study on Judaism. By exploring how Jews struggled to keep Shabbat during the persecution of the Holocaust, students can gain valuable insight into the present day significance of the festival for Jewish families. Some RE teachers draw on the diaries and memories of victims, such as the words of this Jewish teenager remembering Shabbat in the darkness of the Holocaust:

> As the evening drew near, a few of us gathered between the bunks for the Friday evening service. Yes, it was Sabbath again, and as I began to whisper the familiar words of the Sabbath eve Service, I was lulled by the feeling of tranquillity. Gone were the panic and tension that had overwhelmed me these past few days. I discovered for the first time in my life the real power and value of prayer ... here, I knew, was a way of escape, a source of strength and a means of survival of which no power on earth could deprive me. (Tatelbaum, 1985, p. 137)

In religious education students can see how many victims of the Holocaust were able to draw on their shared religious life for inner strength – a kind of spiritual resistance in the face of so much torture and suffering. In many ways the experience of the Holocaust has been interpreted through the symbol and ritual of the Jewish religious community. At Yom Kippur Jews listen to the sung prayer of Kol Nidrei, which is associated with times of persecution; this is now particularly moving for those whose family and friends were destroyed in the Holocaust. Later, in the prayers for Yom Kippur there is a reading from the Book of Jonah. The story is interpreted as a parable about the role of the Jewish people in human suffering. It is also about God's infinite capacity to forgive all humankind – even those who do not in any way deserve to be forgiven. To some extent it is in the context of the ritual life of the Jewish community that the significance of the Holocaust is being worked out; it is in religious education that students can see the ripples of the Holocaust still disturbing the meaning of the rituals and symbols and casting a shadow over the religious life of the Jewish people. Interpreting the religious responses to the Holocaust can encourage students to reflect on the meaning and value of religion, symbol and ritual, encourage them to think about their own response and help them to explore ideas and to find their own way through the terrible stories and events.

Many syllabuses for religious education identify two attainment targets for religious education. The first is 'Learning about Religions' which involves knowledge and understanding of the principal religions and the development of important skills in RE. The second attainment target is 'Learning *from* Religion'. This includes the ability to 'give an informed and considered response to religious and moral issues; reflect on what might be learnt from religions in the light of one's own beliefs and experience; identify and respond to questions of meaning within religions' (QCA, 1998, p. 5).

If pupils approach the Holocaust within the context of RE, the question arises as to what are they learning *from* religion; in other words what have the religious responses to the Holocaust got to offer the young person today who is trying to make sense of or come to terms with the events of the Holocaust? In the examples described above attention has been drawn to the opportunities open to students in the lower secondary school to learn *from* religions and to develop their own resources for working out their personal response to the Holocaust. Older students in religious education can examine Jewish and Christian responses to the Holocaust in a study of Holocaust theology and in looking at the questions that the Holocaust has raised for the different religious communities. In religious education we do not want students to adopt this or that particular religious response but we do want to provide them with the opportunities and resources for reflecting deeply on difficult questions such as those raised by the events of the Holocaust.

In developing learning outcomes for teaching about the Holocaust, teachers identify not only relevant concepts and skills but also certain attitudes that they would hope to develop. Some recent RE syllabuses suggest that attitudes to develop in religious education should include 'an ability to live with ambiguities and paradox; the desire to search for the meaning of life; being prepared to acknowledge bias and prejudice in oneself' (QCA, 1998, p. 6). These are all appropriate in the context of teaching and learning about the Holocaust. On the one hand, the student is required to reflect on the most terrible suffering and evil and, on the other, stories of the most extraordinary courage, self-sacrifice and acts of forgiveness. This requires an ability to live with ambiguities and paradox and in the process of studying the Holocaust, students will confront some of the most challenging questions about life and its meaning. It is in this aspect of teaching and learning about the Holocaust that religious education has an important contribution to make in terms of the spiritual development of students. In the discussion document published for schools on *Spiritual and Moral Development* (National Curriculum Council, (NCC) 1993) teachers are encouraged to look at how their area of the curriculum contributes to the spiritual development of the students. The aspects of spiritual development listed in the guidelines include: 'Search for meaning and purpose – asking "why me" at times of hardship or suffering; reflecting on the origins and purpose of life; responding to challenging experiences of life such as beauty, suffering and death' (NCC, 1993, p. 3).

It is appropriate that religious education should provide the opportunity for reflection on questions about meaning in the face of the events of the Holocaust. Working with other areas of the school curriculum in the study of the Holocaust, RE has an important part to play in terms of developing appropriate attitudes and in terms of contributing to the spiritual development of students.

Many RE teachers believe that one of the attitudes to be developed in religious education is a positive attitude to living in a multicultural and multi-faith society. In some RE syllabuses this is taken to include a willingness 'to acknowledge bias and prejudice in oneself' (QCA, 1998, p. 6). Teachers in religious education often encourage their students to look at the events of the Holocaust in the context of a programme of study on racism and prejudice and some examination courses for GCSE RE include sections on important issues. These courses often include a survey of religious teachings and guidance on issues such as discrimination. For example, students might examine biblical texts such as 'So there is no difference between Jews and Gentiles, between slaves and free people, between men and women; you are all one in union with Christ Jesus' (Galatians 3.28).

The history teacher, like the RE teacher, will want to challenge prejudice and racism; in some schools RE and history work together on teaching about the Holocaust and in looking at the problems of prejudice and racism today. There is some evidence from experimental work in prejudice reduction – for example the work of the Stenhouse project – which suggests that teaching about racism and tackling the problem of prejudice through providing relevant information, through classroom research, debate and discussion can help to combat racist attitudes.

> Teaching about race relations through the strategies studied in this project can, and by and large will, lead to more students moving in the desired direction (less racism) than in the undesired direction (more racism) on a measure of racism. (Stenhouse *et al.*, 1982, p. 275)

The teaching and learning strategies used in the Stenhouse project were working mainly on the cognitive level. Other researchers involved in the field of prejudice reduction in schools have emphasized the emotional aspect of prejudice and recommend programmes that work on both the affective and the cognitive level. It has been suggested that with young children, where prejudice is 'based on a polarised and simple dichotomy of positive versus negative emotions' (Aboud, 1988, p. 132), approaching the problem of prejudice on the affective domain is essential:

> One objective, then, would be to broaden the range of emotions the children are aware of experiencing . . . A second objective would be to teach the children culturally different ways of living and to let them egocentrically and vicariously identify with the happiness and attachments of children from different cultures. (Aboud, 1988, p. 132)

This would suggest that the best way in which RE could contribute to the task of prejudice reduction would be to involve children in exploring the life of different cultures and religious traditions and that this work needs to begin in RE in the primary school. The question has been asked – how do we approach the issue of the Holocaust with primary school students? The answer then is perhaps do not begin with the Holocaust, but begin with work on Judaism. This is the approach taken in the York City Council (1997) teaching resource pack for the Anne Frank Exhibition. It is essential that students receive a positive experience in their study of the Jewish faith if teachers want to challenge prejudice. In primary school, students can learn about the Jewish tradition through the festivals and through looking at Judaism in the home. In joining in a class re-enactment of the festivities of Purim, Hanukkah or Pesach (Passover) they can develop a sense of sharing in some of the experiences of the

Jewish child. In this way religious education can contribute on both the cognitive and affective level and play an essential part in building up a positive encounter with the faith and teachings of the Jewish people. This will help to prepare the ground for later work on the Holocaust.

In teaching about the Holocaust in secondary schools within the context of a scheme of work on racism and prejudice, teachers want to encourage their students to reflect on the lessons for the present day. In doing this they draw on examples of racial discrimination within our own society. A cross-curricular approach offers important opportunities for working on a cognitive as well as an affective level; such an approach might include English and the expressive arts as well as RE and History. Through this broad approach students are able to explore the ways in which racism and prejudice are at work in their own neighbourhood and look at how minorities are vulnerable in our society. The MacPherson (1999) report on the Stephen Lawrence murder inquiry has thrown new light on some of these issues and schools will be advised to explore ways of contributing to the important work of challenging racism. It is important that RE retains a distinctive approach while working with other areas of the curriculum. The history and the English teacher, like the RE teacher, will consider the importance of the moral development of the students when looking at the Holocaust. In all these subjects the teacher wants to raise awareness of just where racial hatred and prejudice can lead; the aims in terms of moral education are therefore much the same. Religious education has an important part to play in keeping the spiritual as well as the moral dimension in focus. Spiritual does not have to mean explicitly religious. In his chapter 'Education, spirituality and the whole child: a humanist perspective', John White (1996) encourages the teacher to consider an important aspect of spirituality. He quotes from the words from J.B. Priestley's (1947) *An Inspector Calls* and argues that as well as a sense of injustice, teachers need to develop in their students a sense of community. This is in fact one aspect of spirituality given in the National Curriculum Council discussion document:

> Just remember this. One Eva Smith has died – but there are millions and millions and millions of Eva Smiths and John Smiths still left with us, with their lives, their hopes and fears, their suffering and chance of happiness, all intertwined with our lives, with what we think and say and do. We don't live alone. We are members of one body. We are responsible for each other.

What better way of stimulating our young people 'to the sense of injustice: developing a sense of community: valuing the worth of each individual' – all aspects of spiritual development set out in the NCC document (White, 1996, p. 39).

White was speaking from the perspective of an English teacher; he could just as well have been writing from the perspective of the RE teacher – as religious education has an important part to play in encouraging students to develop a sense of community. For many involved in teaching RE there is a concern to develop a sense of the oneness of humankind – a sense of oneness which is able to embrace diversity – the diversity of cultures, religions and beliefs which make up the world in which we live. There is a sense in which good religious education – whether the focus is Judaism, Islam, Hinduism or Sikhism, or the different traditions within Christianity – is contributing to the work of Holocaust education because it aims through the study of religion to 'develop a positive attitude towards other people, respecting their right to hold beliefs different from their own, and towards living in a society of diverse religions' (QCA, 1998, p. 2).

REFERENCES

Aboud, F. (1988) *Children and Prejudice*. Oxford: Basil Blackwell.

Bayfield, T. (1981) *Churban: The Murder of the Jews of Europe*. London: Michael Goulston Educational Foundation.

London Borough of Croydon (LBC) (1992) *A New Agreed Syllabus for RE in Croydon Schools*. London: LBC.

MacPherson, W. (1999) *The Stephen Lawrence Inquiry*. London: Stationery Office.

Manchester City Council (MCC) Education Department (1996) *Agreed Syllabus in Religious Education*. Manchester: MCC.

National Curriculum Council (NCC) (1993) *Spiritual and Moral Development*. York: NCC.

Qualifications and Curriculum Authority (QCA) (1998) *Model Syllabuses for Religious Education*. London: QCA.

Stenhouse, L., Verma, G.K., Wild, R.D. and Nixon, J. (1982) *Teaching about Race Relations: Problems and Effects in British Schools*. London: Routledge and Kegan Paul.

Supple, C. (1992) *From Prejudice to Genocide: Learning about the Holocaust*. Stoke-on-Trent: Trentham Books.

Tatelbaum, I. (1985) *Through our Eyes*. Jerusalem: IBT Publishing.

White, J. (1996) Education, spirituality and the whole child: a humanist perspective. In R. Best (ed.) *Education, Spirituality and the Whole Child*. London: Cassell.

York City Council (1997) *Anne Frank: A History for Today. Beliefs, Racism and Prejudice. Teachers' Resource Pack*. York: City of York Council Educational Services.

Chapter 12

Teaching the Holocaust through an Educational Exhibition

Ian Davies, Ian Gregory and Andrew Lund

CONTEXT

Previous work (e.g. Short, 1995) has referred to the curious position which teaching and learning about the Holocaust occupies. Given the undeniable significance of the Holocaust as well as concerns arising from the current political context and young people's understandings of contemporary life (Council of Europe, 1996; de Laine, 1997) it is very important to ensure that the Holocaust is taught appropriately and effectively. And yet, although a range of organizations exist to promote such work (such as the Holocaust Educational Trust) and while some resources are available for teachers (Supple, 1992), the work in schools is often low status with little time devoted to it (Brown and Davies, 1998). In the face of these difficulties it is perhaps necessary to search for a supplementary (not alternative) way to help teachers and pupils go beyond the work they might normally undertake within school.

The supplementary way forward investigated here is through involvement with a travelling educational exhibition. The exhibition of the Anne Frank Educational Trust (together with associated events) visited York during the period 5–30 January 1998. This Anne Frank exhibition was launched in 1996 by the current British Prime Minister Tony Blair. The previous version of the exhibition (1985–96) was visited by 7 million visitors in total. The current exhibition aims to inform visitors about history, show differences between people, encourage tolerance and mutual respect and convince people that a society in which differences are respected does not come about unaided.

We argue that use of such a facility may provide, generally, a very positive educational way forward.

METHODOLOGY

We did not see ourselves as operating within some sort of spuriously objective and amoral framework. Without, of course, avoiding difficult questions, it was envisaged at the outset that the research project would promote an awareness of the importance of the need to teach for the reduction of prejudice and discrimination, develop our understanding of teaching and learning about Anne Frank and similar topics and allow for an opportunity to consider the strategies which will aid the professional development of teachers. Three researchers established a case study approach using techniques associated with condensed fieldwork in which perceptions of pupils, teachers and organizers were explored.

The core of data was gathered from ten case study schools, which reflected a range of types of school with additional material from other schools and members of the public. Different data collection points were used to cover work before, during and after the exhibition. The types and amounts of data gathered are listed in Table 12.1. Raw data were interpreted separately and then discussed by the researchers.

Table 12.1 *Types and amounts of data gathered*

Types of data	Number of responses
Interviews with organizers (45–60 minutes each, taped and transcribed)	5
Observations at the exhibition (each of at least one hour)	18
Classroom observations (each of at least 30 minutes)	7
Pupil questionnaires	146
Visitors' book entries (representing many more people than the number shown here as there were many comments made on behalf of families or other groups)	1669
Responses to the museum services feedback sheet	278

KEY THEMES

Organization of and preparation for the exhibition

In autumn 1997 a series of five meetings of a steering committee took place with sixteen members including the Director of Educational Services. A separate education committee was established with the RE adviser taking responsibility for its co-ordination. Teaching packs were produced which gave suggestions as to what to do before, during and after a visit to the exhibition. Teachers were invited to a preparatory session at the exhibition. Publicity for the event was directed locally and beyond. At least some of the guides felt that 'the organization was slightly lax'. There was also a problem perceived by some relating to the time needed to see the exhibition, with different periods being seen as necessary for a visit by the Trust and those responsible for taking bookings.

The very success of the exhibition in attracting large numbers of people seemed to lessen the impact of the exhibition for some. Some of the teachers regarded the mingling of pupils and public as a good thing (a member of the education committee commented: 'I think it's good for school kids to see it with others'); others had wrongly assumed that they had exclusive access for the period booked. The associated events had elements of success. The official opening began with a reading from the *Diary of Anne Frank* by a teenage girl. Other associated events were well received.

A medieval guildhall in the city centre housed the exhibition. It was accessible and generally regarded as being suitable, although a few objected that many of the merchants who had used the hall would have profited from slavery, which has been compared to the Holocaust. Similarly, the projection of images of Anne Frank herself and other relevant pictures on to Clifford's Tower were seen by a few as being tasteless given that the tower was the site of the deaths of many Jews during the twelfth century following antisemitic demonstrations. However, most when questioned suggested that it was good that the life of Anne Frank had helped to transform the sites into 'respectable' places.

The visitors

Over 15,000 people visited the exhibition. The numbers and types of school parties with numbers of pupils and teachers are shown in Table 12.2.

Table 12.2   *Numbers and types of visitors*

Focus	Groups	Schools	Pupils and teachers
Combined subject (primary school)	10	8	286
Combined subject (special school)	11	6	119
Religious education (secondary school)	13	5	363
History (secondary school)	33	12	1070
English (secondary school)	3	3	104
Other	6	3	98
Unknown	3	2	90
Total	79	39	2130

It is doubtful that more people could have been accommodated. However, of the 39 schools visiting the exhibition only 14 were from within the host LEA. Of these schools only 6 of the 12 secondaries, 6 of the primaries and 2 special schools attended (from a total of 79 schools). Perhaps those who did not attend felt that the exhibition would already be too crowded. As most of the case study schools attended opportunistically and made alterations to their teaching programmes at short notice, it is possible that some felt that the disadvantages to students' learning would outweigh any potential advantages to be gained by visiting the exhibition. There is also slight evidence that some schools were put off by the travelling distance and difficulties of gaining supply cover. For a period of approximately one hour, and for an exhibition which could comfortably accommodate only approximately 50 pupils at any one time, attendance would mean relatively significant commitments in terms of both time and money.

The largest proportion of school visitors to the exhibition were within Years 8 to 10 (age 12–15) with most pupils from Year 9 (13–14 years old). Teachers had to consider pupils' emotional capacity to make appropriate responses and pupils' intellectual ability. There were examples of teachers fearing inappropriate responses from the less able. There was, however, no real pattern to this. One case study school decided to take only less able children to the exhibition as it was felt that the 'bottom set' would not 'respond appropriately' to the

Jewish culture/music event that the rest of Year 10 were to attend. By contrast, a teacher from another case study school explained that she had some concerns about the pupils who had chosen to go to the exhibition. She had originally targeted a top set but very few had volunteered:

> I've just been along to the class where 3 out of the 30 are coming. I've just been to say how disappointed I am ... OK, I might be misjudging those kids in the lower sets ... what I'm hoping is that they are not using it as an excuse to get out of school for the day ... I think it's more of interest to top set kids. (secondary teacher)

Some of the teachers remarked that the language used on the exhibition panels and by the guides was too complex. However, most of the case study schools decided to take all pupils in a year group. There was overwhelmingly positive behaviour and appropriate responses by pupils. There were no major differences between the responses of boys and girls either at the exhibition or through questionnaire responses.

VISITORS' RESPONSES

An Anne Frank exhibition

Most respondents felt that Anne's life had been represented in a valuable manner with 69 per cent of the pupils responding to the questionnaire by either strongly agreeing or agreeing that they 'liked the way the exhibition showed Anne's life'. Also, there was a very strong perception that the teaching of the Holocaust had been given a new dimension. Anne Frank is seen as a way into understanding the Holocaust and related key ideas about religion, history, politics and individual experience without exposing children to overly complex or horrifically graphic images. Teachers from four of the case study schools explicitly said that this change of emphasis would be long lasting with a change made to programmes of study.

> she talks about events they can easily relate to and then this awful thing happens. We don't go into this in great detail. But it is an empathy. It is relevant to PSE [personal and social education] which we have got quite a strong focus on that in the school. There is the RE side of things, the fact that Anne Frank was a young Jewish girl who lived in a community that was not tolerated because it was Jewish. (primary teacher)

Some teachers felt that the exhibition did well to avoid horrific images:

> I liked the fact that it kept off the horrors. It dealt with the terrible loss of a
> young life and her hopes and ideals and I think other children like that. The
> horror of it came out through that rather than [through the use of terrible
> images]. (member of education committee)

The above was not a unanimous view. Some teachers felt that without
the horror of the Holocaust its real message cannot be grasped. The
questionnaire results from pupils are not entirely clear. Although
only 24 per cent disagreed or strongly disagreed with the proposition
that the exhibition had shown 'about the right amount of shocking
pictures about the Holocaust', the positive view was not over-
whelming, with only 57 per cent agreeing or strongly agreeing with
the statement. There was no sense from the way the questionnaires
had been completed that pupils were seeking to make provocative
and unacceptable points in a search for unpleasant images.

In another important way the exhibition was perceived to help
overcome some very significant barriers. Recent academic developments have tended to emphasize the micro-historical approach and
this may allow for an improved understanding of large-scale events.
'There is a quotation in the exhibition the Holocaust wasn't the
murder of six million people it was the murder of one person six
million times over' (Trust member). The story of Anne Frank may be
very valuable as the fate of the individuals shows that they could not
have done more and so at least implies the power – rather than the
potential neglect – of structural considerations.

Furthermore, the representation of a life within a family can be dealt
with only by using insights from a number of different sources. The visit
to the Anne Frank exhibition was usually led by individual curricular
specialists and there was evidence of teachers still finding it hard to work
very closely with other teachers. However, teachers did work together to
promote, very explicitly, various human insights in what is much more
than simple cross-curricular understanding. What still needs further
exploration is the extent to which a particular view of the past and how
it should be represented interacts with the pedagogical approach which
is adopted. Put simply, in using Anne Frank as a pedagogical device do
teachers necessarily promote a view on how history is made, or will the
device always remain merely an instrument to achieve whatever sort of
historical understanding is preferred by a teacher?

The representation of Jewish lives and beliefs

The emphasis on Judaism was noticeable and was perceived as being
appropriate. Many of the school groups who visited the exhibition
were led by RE teachers. The primary pack for teachers and children

had been written from an RE perspective. Work on that pack had been submitted in draft form to representatives from the Jewish community. However, there were limits placed on the focus on Judaism. There were some who while wanting a proper explanation of key events and beliefs within a liberal framework were pleased that this limiting approach was employed:

> I thought I was very impressed with the Jewish person [the leader of the introductory evening for teachers]. I think [dealing with] antisemitism that is fair enough but it can go the other way and become pro Jewish and that is why I appreciate his particular approach. He kept saying 'right, this is about this particular girl who was a Jew but you've got all this type of problem still in the world today and it's not just confined to antisemitism there's racism there's sexism' and he did keep referring to this. (secondary teacher)

The representation of the past and present

The largest number of school groups attending the exhibition said that the main focus of their visit related to history. Almost all interviewees said that the minimum preparation would relate to the development of awareness of the historical context. A member of the Trust said that

> [the guides] have to have more depth of knowledge ... They have to understand something about the history of the period; that this was a set of circumstances that came about after the First World War; how that came about; why that came about; the economic situation. (Trust member)

However, the exhibition did not deal with the long-term history of antisemitism in any depth; there was disagreement within the Trust itself as to whether the exhibition dealt with the history of the Nazi Germany effectively. There were no very clear views from pupils as to whether this historical material had been dealt with adequately: 53 per cent of respondents to the questionnaire agreed or strongly agreed that the history of Nazi Germany had been explained clearly; the remainder saying they did not know or disagreed.

The representation of the key events and issues carried important issues relating to the relationship between past and present. It was explained that the exhibition had been designed so that 'In the pavilions you walk in and all around you there is the time and place whether it's Anne Frank's bedroom or a Nazi rally – you're there. But round the back of each pavilion this is now 'I was there' (Trust member)

Thus there is a rather sophisticated interplay between a narrative which is organized into key dates with experiential opportunities, while the contemporary focus is present throughout. This interplay between past and present was given an added dimension by the use of three separate panels which focused on contemporary images (including reference to Stephen Lawrence and others who had faced injustice at school or elsewhere).

However, respondents said that they were not aware of this interplay, that the guides had not referred to it, and said that there were problems with such an approach. The issue of space and the placing of the panels was important for the route that was taken by visitors. Some suggested that the simple need to fit the panels into a specific physical space was more important than the development of a particular arrangement to fit a particular message or set of ideas. Although the panels had been numbered, visitors (and, on some occasions, guides) did not find it easy to follow a clear route. The panels on gypsies had been placed very close to a wall which led to one respondent noting: 'there did not seem much on gypsies and the bits that were tucked round an angle where people weren't seeing them unfortunately' (member of education committee).

Pupils were placed in small groups and led through different routes. The reasons for the routes taken arose from practical rather than pedagogical considerations. We do not have clear evidence as to any differences which may have resulted. There were, however, firmly held preferences among respondents as to the best way to proceed, with some suggesting that an historical overview had to be presented first, with others wanting an explanation of contemporary events at the outset.

For some there was a need to develop real action in a wider political context. For example:

> I think it's very important when children recognize that when they see things about Bosnia on the television they can say to themselves 'well, we really can't allow this to happen or our government can't allow it to happen'. (City of York representative)

However, most people felt that political action should be avoided. The exhibition organizers were wary of building in an action dimension to the exhibition:

> we are handing it over; we are giving ownership for that period to a group of people who come together for that purpose in the city. At any one time there are 12–15 Anne Frank committees around the country planning the exhibition to bring it to their community .... It is very much in their hands. (Trust member)

Most teachers used the exhibition not to make wide-ranging political points but rather to promote an awareness of Anne Frank and of how they might become aware of and avoid inflicting in their own ways sufferings upon others. It seemed that messages relating to interpersonal relationships were seen as being more emphasized than anything which was more obviously and explicitly political. Nearly two-thirds (62 per cent) of pupils did not know, disagreed or strongly disagreed with the proposition that 'I think the exhibition has encouraged me to do something either now or in the future'.

WORK RELATING TO THE EXHIBITION: BEFORE, DURING AND AFTER A VISIT

For preparatory work in the ten case study schools there was a roughly equal balance between those who chose to prepare specifically for this exhibition and those who were able only to explain how the exhibition linked with work which had or would be undertaken. For some the aims were rather general (for example to raise standards through fieldwork or to promote history as a subject within the school). Most schools were simply acting opportunistically in the light of a desire to go to a travelling exhibition on an important topic which was relevant to school work and to school life. On one occasion the school was teaching Judaism at the time of the exhibition and some of the history focused visits took place after an explanation of the events of the 1930s but others had, for example, taught Judaism in the previous term, read the *Diary of Anne Frank* last year or planned to teach the Second World War during the summer term. Of the pupils who responded to the questionnaire 70 per cent said that they agreed or strongly agreed with the statement 'The exhibition has helped me to understand better the work we did at school'. However, teachers did not appear to be convinced of the need to develop precise objectives. This seemed to be due to a wariness of objectives which could potentially be inappropriate in an experience which did not merely have the normal cognitive aims of specialist academic work in schools.

The relationship between the teachers and the guides was significant. Some of the guides had personal experience of the issues associated with the Second World War. The work of the guides was handled on the whole with success. Clear explanations and obvious commitment were clearly in evidence on a number of occasions. However, on some – but by no means all – occasions teachers felt that the guides were not able to demonstrate the standard of teaching which they had expected. Some teachers felt that the guides had made insufficient links with the contemporary situation, or failed to provide enough contextual explanation for the rise of the Nazis.

Some teachers said that some guides made historical errors. The time made available for different parts of the tours was criticized with the video showing being interrupted, and at other times there being too much time for unstructured observing. Guides were seen to use only three main types of questions: a check on the understanding of vocabulary, an encouragement for pupils to show that they had identified dates or names shown on the panels, and allowing pupils to ask their own questions. A minority of guides lacked basic presentational skills. These criticisms should not be seen as invalidating the very successful work achieved generally. There is the possibility that the teachers were at times discussing a different way of working which they preferred rather than a way which was necessarily better for all. There is great value in having guides to support teachers. However, one of the guides explained:

> part of the problem was that they [teachers] assumed that the guides were actually attached to the exhibition itself, travel around and knew everything in depth which of course, we did our best, but we don't know everything in depth. (guide)

The nature of follow-up work varied. Some teachers focused on whole school issues such as bullying; some children produced files on Anne Frank and Nazi Germany in history lessons; others discussed the visit; one school held a brief discussion and then took pupils around the railway museum as they were visiting from outside the LEA and felt the need to make the most of the day; some schools did not follow up at all.

Thus there seems to be teachers making arrangements with little lead-in time, with some doing no preparation with children and handing the learning process to some people who were not experts on the particular historical period or did not have sufficient related experience or skills. While the teacher adopting the role of expert can have negative aspects, there seem to be some grounds for suggesting a clearer structure for such work which would allow greater collaboration to grow between the partners.

CONCLUSION

The visit of the Anne Frank exhibition to York was a very clear success. Specifically, the exhibition itself was seen as being very valuable; the event was well organized; the material produced for teachers was good; there was a large number of visitors who clearly gained a great deal from the experience. There was clear and successful co-operation between many different organizations and individuals.

However, there are a number of points which need to be addressed if the use of an educational exhibition is to be seen as providing an important supplementary part of pupils' experiences. First, the reasons for the limited number of schools visiting from within the host local education authority need to be explored. The timing of the visit of the exhibition and associated forward planning may need to be questioned. Perhaps the approach used by the City of Birmingham in which necessary pupil experiences (as well as the usual learning objectives) are a part of curriculum planning could provide a way forward. Second, teachers' thinking about the suitability of work on Anne Frank for particular pupils needs to be investigated. At the moment there seems to be a rough consensus that secondary school pupils studying history and (to a lesser extent) RE form the most common target group. The reasons for this are not entirely clear. The relationships between age, cognitive capacity and emotional maturity are felt implicitly, rather than understood. Third, the amount and type of knowledge needed by pupils is not clear. It seems that some historical background is a key requirement but little preparation was undertaken by some teachers. The relationship between different types of teachers and exhibition guides is probably in need of some work as currently the former may expect too much of the latter and teachers of different subject areas undertake little co-operative work. Fourth, the way in which the Holocaust is represented is obviously controversial. There are differing views on the relative weight to be given to the different types of victims (Jews, homosexuals and others); on whether it is a unique event; on the relationship between past and present and the extent to which contemporary issues can be explored. Fifth, pedagogical debates (which relate to issues of how the Holocaust should be represented) centre on the relative emphasis to be given to Anne Frank as a means of understanding large-scale events; the use of horrific images; the use of chronological narrative as opposed to more thematic analysis; the boundaries which may need to be set if attempts are made, even in a limited way, to develop a sense of 'being there'; and the ways in which issues arising from learning in particular contexts (such as in a relatively monocultural York) should be developed by teachers.

The above questions and issues are fundamental to the development of better understanding of the Holocaust, better teaching and learning and hopefully allow for the possibility of the development of a society in which groups and individuals are more aware of their responsibilities to promote and defend social justice. As such these points are meant to commend the work of the Anne Frank Educational Trust and of people within York for hosting the exhibition, and to encourage them to continue the search for even better thinking and practice.

REFERENCES

Brown, M. and Davies, I. (1998) The Holocaust and education for citizenship: the teaching of history, religion and human rights in England, *Educational Review*, **50**(1): 75–83.

Council of Europe (1996) *History Teaching and the Promotion of Democratic Values and Tolerance: A Handbook for Teachers*. Strasbourg, Council of Europe.

De Laine, M. (1997) Third of teenagers deny Holocaust. *The Times Educational Supplement*, 4 July, 18.

Short, G. (1995) The Holocaust in the National Curriculum: a survey of teachers' attitudes and practices, *Journal of Holocaust Education*, **4**, 167–88.

Supple, C. (1992) *From Prejudice to Genocide: Learning about the Holocaust*. Stoke-on-Trent: Trentham Books.

Index

Aboud, F.   159
Abram, I.   74
Abs, H. J.   68
Abulafia, A. S.   21
Adorno, T. W.   73, 77
affective-cognitive continuum   5, 160
Alexandria   14
Andrews, R.   123, 127
Antioch   15
antisemitism   2, 11, 28, 29, 39, 42,
     54, 55, 68, 77, 95, 110, 137, 165,
     169
Anne Frank
   Centre   111
   Diary   35, 94, 96, 105, 143, 165,
      171
   Educational Trust   1, 6, 108, 147,
      159, 163 *passim* (esp. 67–8)
Arendt, H.   51, 142
Atkinson, J.   124
Auschwitz   2, 26, 40, 41, 43, 64, 68,
     69, 71, 73, 77–91, 111, 142, 144,
     153

Bain, R.   124
Baines, B.   109
Bale, A.   18
Bari   16
Baron, S. W.   12
Bauer, Y.   42
Bauman, Z.   3
Bayfield, T.   153
Beinart, H.   13, 17, 18, 19
Birkenau   77–91
Blackburne, L.   136
Blishen, E.   119
Braun, R.   3
Bresheeth, H.   107
Brooman, J.
Brown, M.   4, 5, 163
Browning, C. L.   3, 5, 143
Buber, M.   74
Buchignani, W.   105

Burleigh, M.   42, 107
Burston, H.   135

Carter, R.   123, 127
Carthage   14
Chazan, R.   17, 18
'choiceless choices'   54
consequentialist accounts   49
Constantine   13, 14
Council of Europe   4, 163
Cox, B.   124
Croydon   151

Davies, I.   4, 5, 1–8, 163–74, 163
Dawidowicz, L.   43, 95, 96, 97
De Laine, M.   4, 136, 163
De Marco, N.   109
definition of the Holocaust   63
democratic accountability   6, 57, 101,
     122–5
Dentith, S.   122, 123
Department for Education   123
Department of Education and Science
     123
Dobson, R. B.   11, 17, 18, 21

Educational (research/professional/
     policy) organizations
   Anne Frank Educational Trust   1, 6,
      108, 147, 159, 163 *passim*
   Holocaust Educational Trust   163
   Institute of Contemporary History
      and Wiener Library   109
   National Association for the Teaching
      of English   126
   QCA (Qualifications and Curriculum
      Authority)   27, 31, 34, 152, 156,
      157–8, 161
   School Curriculum and Assessment
      Authority (SCAA)   113
   Spiro Institute   108
Edwards, J.   13, 14, 21
electronic communication   127

England   2, 105–15
  Education Reform Act (1988)   105, 106
Engle, S.   101
English (school subject/academic discipline)   2, 6
Ephesus   14
Esther   34

Facing History and Ourselves   94–6, 103
Fackenheim, E.   39
fictional portrayals   94, 102, 105
  Michaels, A.   3
  Richter, H. P.   5, 105
  Schlink, B.   3
Fine, M.   95
Fletcher, R.   14, 16, 17
forgiveness   154 *passim*
Forta, A.   110
Foster, S.   2, 6, 7, 25–36, 151–61
Fox, J. P.   105

Geras, N.   56
Germans, Germany   2, 18, 19, 40, 42, 44, 55, 63–76, 101, 169
  Berlin Wall   4
  Bitburg   3
  Federal Republic of Germany   66, 67–9
  German Democratic Republic   65–7
Gilbert, M.   142, 143, 144, 145
Ginzberg, C.   14, 15, 16
Golb, N.   20
Goldhagen, D.   5, 42, 45, 64, 143
Gregory, I.   2, 6, 37–47, 49–59, 163–74
Grey, P.   109
'Gypsies'   42, 43, 63, 64, 72, 97
  Roma   63, 64, 67, 81, 83, 130
  Sinti   63, 64, 67

Hadrian   13
Halliday, M. A. K.   127
Hampshire, S.   46
Harris, M.   113
Hartman, G.   3
Haydn, T.   2, 135–49
Heaney, S.   131
Hector, S.   2, 105–15, 107, 108, 112
Heimer, E.   120
Hentig, H. von   73

Herrnstein, R.   145
Heyl, M.   74
Hilberg, R.   38
Hill, G.   131–2
history   2, 6, 11–23, 44, 50, 53–4, 74, 79, 83, 168–9
homosexuals   43, 51, 67, 72, 173
hope   56, 59, 75
horrific images   73–4, 168
Hunt, M.   144

inappropriate responses   166
incomprehensibility   39, 41–6, 49, 136, 154
individual identity   28, 78, 143
indoctrination   124
intellectual issues   1–2, 37–47, 49–59
intentionalist–functionalist debate   54
international overviews   62–115
Israel   51, 68

Jaspers, K.   38
Jenkins, J.   110
Jewish background   25–36, 81
Jewish Diaspora   13
Jewish Education Bureau   111
Jewish history   12 *passim*
  Maccabees   15
Jews   12, 13, 14, 20, 64, 81, 113, 120
  segregation of Jewish communities   19
Journal of Holocaust Education   111
Judaea   13
Judaism   2, 25–36, 110, 156, 168–9, 171
  anti-Judaism   15
  Askenazi   20, 33
  Hasid   12, 20, 21
  kosher   28, 152
  Pesach (Passover)   13, 34, 35, 159
  pogroms   17
  Purim   34, 155
  Sephardic   20, 33
  Shabbat   28, 32, 156
  Talmud   21, 31
Judd, J.   130
Justinian Code   14

Kabbalah   21
Kalfus, R.   101
Karpf, A.   3, 143
Katz, J.   12, 20, 21

Kelly, N.   109
Kerr, J.   105, 109
Kinloch, N.   4
Klein, R.   108
Klemperer, V.   64, 74
knowledge about the Holocaust   136
Kochan, L.   107, 110
Kohlberg, L.   139
Kristallnacht   4, 28, 121
Kussatz, S.   63–76

Laird, C.   105
Landau, R.   5, 58, 107, 121, 122,
    128
Lane Fox, R.   14
Lang, B.   51
Langer, L.   54, 56
Langmuir, G. I.   11
Language   119–22
Lanham, R.   127, 131
Leavis, F. R.   125, 126, 128
Lee, D.   119
Lee, P.   138
Lindemann, A. S.   11, 12, 18, 20, 21
Lipstadt, D.   96
Little, R.   109
Lovelace, A.   110
Lund, A.   2, 6, 163–74

McGuinn, N.   2, 6, 119–33
Magurshak, D.   53
Manchester   151
Marrus, M.   121
Mathieson, M.   124
Meade, F. H. M.   31
Medway, P.   125
memorial sites   75, 98
    Beth Shalom   108
    Yad Veshem   111
    see also Auschwitz
Mercier, C.   2, 6, 7, 25–36, 151–61
Middle Ages   16–20
Milchman, A.   3
Minorca   16
Misnah   31
modern history   20–1
modern state   55
morality   40, 45–6, 50, 52, 55, 56, 78,
    80, 81, 137
Mortkowitz, S.   130
Murray, C.   145

Museums
    Beit Hashoah Museum of Tolerance,
        Los Angeles   94
    Imperial War Museum   108
    United States Holocaust Memorial
        Museum   93, 94, 98–9, 100, 103,
        111, 137

narrative   140–1
Nazis, Nazism   37, 38, 43, 51, 55, 56,
    58, 64–65, 82, 120 *passim*; 141
    Wannsee conference   64
Nero   13
Niewyk, D. L.   100
Nixon, J.   159
Noctor, M.   109

Ochoa, A.   101
O'Kane, R. H. T.   3
Oleksy, K.   2, 77–91
O'Neill, J.   102
'ordinary people'   79, 101, 143, 153

Pagis, D.   102
Palestine   17
Parkes, J. W.   13, 14, 15
Parsons, W. S.   98, 99, 101, 102
Partington, G.   144
pedagogical issues
    assessment   100
    citizenship education   106
    controversial issues   50–1
    English teaching   94, 102, 119–33,
        160–1
    general   2, 4, 52, 100–1, 125–6
    history teaching   53, 57, 58, 72, 83,
        94, 96, 105, 106, 107–9, 135–49, 172
    internet   99, 103, 111, 146
    moral education   57, 106
    religious education   2, 6, 30–6, 72,
        151–61, 106, 109–11, 151–61, 169
    resources   110–11
    study day   112
    teacher education   81–4
    time for teaching   4, 96, 107, 113, 163
    using an exhibition   98–9, 108,
        163–74
    video   86, 108, 111, 147
    visiting memorial sites   75, 77–91,
        108
people with disabilities   43, 63, 72, 145

Poland   2, 41, 43, 77 *passim*
political dimension   6, 29, 40, 57, 95,
      122–5, 170–1
Purves, A. C.   102

questions   138–40, 172

racism   43, 46, 52, 77, 98, 106, 151, 160
   Lawrence, Stephen   106, 160, 170
   MacPherson, W.   160
   prejudice   1, 30, 49, 55, 58, 83, 96,
      159
   stereotyping   30–1, 110
Radway, R.   109
Rathenow, H-F.   2, 63–76
Reagan, R. (US President)   3
Rees-Jones, S.   2, 11–23
relevance   136, 142, 146
religion   18, 25–36,
   religious persecution   155
   religious prejudice   83
representations of the Holocaust   3–4
responsibility   40, 57, 80, 95, 145, 173–4
Rico, G. L.   100
Roman Empire   13–16
Rorty, R.   59
Rosenberg, A.   3

Sacks, J.   26,
Shoah   64, 152
Short, G.   4, 110, 113, 163–74
significance   3, 38, 55, 59, 143–4
Sobol, M.   94
societal issues   4
Spain   18, 20
Steinburg, 145
Stenhouse, L.   159
Stow, K.   13, 14, 15, 17, 18, 19, 20, 21
Stradling, R.   109
Strom, M. S.   101, 102
'suffering history'   12
Sukkot   34

Supple, C.   5, 58, 107, 120, 138, 153, 163
survivors   89, 114, 140
Swann   35

Tatelbaum, I.   28, 156
Technology   55
Tenakh   32
texts   128–32
Theodosian Code   14, 15
Thompson, D.   125–6, 128
Titus   13
tolerance   5, 51, 161
Torah   14, 27, 28, 31, 33, 152
Totten, S.   2, 93–104, 98, 99, 100, 101,
      102

uniqueness   3, 12, 39, 42, 49, 98, 146
United States   2, 64, 70, 93–104
   Beit Hashoah Museum of Tolerance,
      Los Angeles   94
   United States Holocaust Memorial
      Museum   93, 94, 98–9, 100, 103,
      111, 137

Verma, G. K.   159

White, J.   110, 124, 160–1
Whittock, M.   109
whole school initiatives   126
Wiesel, E.   96, 111, 153
Wiesenthal, S.   51
Wieser, P.   101
Wild, R. D.   159
Wilkins, C.   4
Wipperman, W.   107

Yemenite   33
Yom Kippur   156, 157
York   1, 11, 17, 18, 21, 147, 159,
      163–74

Zimmerman, A. W.   31